19 Chapelle

18 BD. DE LA CHAPELLE

11 BD. DE MAGENTA   Buttes-Chaumont

Belleville

2 Marais   BD. VOLTAIRE

Bastille

12

13 **14**

RUE DE RIVOLI

arter

3

4   THE RIVER SEINE

3 PLACE MONGE

4 RUE MOUFFETARD

5 RASPAIL

6 LA GRANDE ÉPICERIE

7 SAXE-BRETEUIL

8 RUE CLER

9 BATIGNOLLES

10 GALERIES LAFAYETTE

11 SAINT-QUENTIN

12 BASTILLE

13 BEAUVAU

14 RUE D'ALIGRE

15 EDGAR QUINET

16 GRENELLE

17 PRÉSIDENT WILSON

18 BARBÈS

19 LA CHAPELLE

MARKETS
OF PARIS

Markets $\overline{\text{OF}}$ Paris

SECOND EDITION

DIXON LONG & MARJORIE R. WILLIAMS

PHOTOGRAPHS BY MARJORIE R. WILLIAMS

THE LITTLE BOOKROOM
NEW YORK

© 2012 The Little Bookroom
Text © 2012 Dixon Long and Marjorie R. Williams
Photos © 2012 Marjorie R. Williams

Cover and Endpaper Illustration Susan Burghart

Library of Congress Cataloging-in-Publication Data

Long, Dixon.
Markets of Paris / by Dixon Long and Marjorie R. Williams ;
photographs by Marjorie R. Williams.–2nd ed.
p. cm.
Includes bibliographical references and index.
ISBN 978-1-936941-00-1 (alk. paper)
1. Markets–France–Paris–Guidebooks. 2. Paris (France)–
Guidebooks. I. Williams, Marjorie R. II. Title.
HF5474.F9P34 2012
381'.180944361--dc23
2011041982

Printed in the United States of America
10 9 8 7 6 5 4 3 2 1

Published by The Little Bookroom
435 Hudson Street, Suite 300
New York NY 10014
editorial@littlebookroom.com
www.littlebookroom.com

To the memories of Ruthanne Long and Gloria Williams
whose love of travel, people, food, and adventure live on

———————◆———————

Paris is always a good idea.
(Audrey Hepburn in the film *Sabrina*)

CONTENTS

INTRODUCTION • 10

PRACTICAL SUGGESTIONS • 13

GETTING ALONG IN THE FOOD MARKETS • 17

IF YOU HAVE LIMITED TIME • 21

✦

1st *arrondissement* • LOUVRE • 23

2nd *arrondissement* • BOURSE • 33

3rd *arrondissement* • MARAIS • 49

4th *arrondissement* • ISLANDS IN THE SEINE • 51

5th *arrondissement* • LATIN QUARTER • 59

6th *arrondissement* • SAINT-GERMAIN • 71

7th *arrondissement* • EIFFEL TOWER • 87

8th *arrondissement* • CHAMPS-ÉLYSÉES • 103

9th *arrondissement* • OPÉRA • 117

10th *arrondissement* • GARE DU NORD • 135

11th *arrondissement* • BASTILLE • 143

12th *arrondissement* • BERCY • 153

13th *arrondissement* • NATIONAL LIBRARY • 169

14th *arrondissement* • MONTPARNASSE • 177

15th *arrondissement* • VAUGIRARD • 199

16th *arrondissement* • TROCADÉRO • 213

17th *arrondissement* • BATIGNOLLES • 225

18th *arrondissement* • MONTMARTRE • 231

19th *arrondissement* • BUTTES-CHAUMONT • 249

20th *arrondissement* • BELLEVILLE • 255

✦

EATING OUT IN PARIS • 265

RESTAURANTS • 267

HELPFUL BOOKS, BLOGS, AND WEBSITES • 285

OPEN ON SUNDAY • 288

RESTAURANT INDEX • 292

MARKET INDEX • 295

Introduction

We have a love affair with markets. For Dixon, it began when he lived in Paris in the 1960s and found that flea markets were the best places to buy inexpensive furniture and household goods. For Marjorie, it began when she visited Fontainebleau in 1995 and heard the early morning buzz build as a market took shape in the plaza across from her hotel. For both of us, the discovery of Paris's open-air food markets transformed that affair into a long-term relationship. The abundance of good things to cook and to eat, their freshness, and the good will of the vendors, gathered us in an embrace that never let us go.

Why do markets dazzle and delight us? Above all, it's the opportunity to observe and participate in an experience that is quintessentially French, and independent of social or economic class. In the markets, real people fill real needs for food, clothing, tools, household goods—sustenance for the body—but also books, stamps, letters, and relics from the past that nurture the mind and the soul. Moreover, there's no requirement for the observer to participate (though you may strike up a conversation or two). In a market, you're plunged into an authentic experience in which you can be as anonymous as you wish, or speak up to anyone you happen to rub elbows with.

As we define it, a market is a place where you can find a lot of the same thing at competitive prices. There is a market in Paris for fabrics, and another for paper ephemera goods. Birds and small animals have markets of their own. Similar kinds of shops have migrated to common locations that function as markets—for example, antiques, ceramics, fine art, textiles, musical instruments, and overstocked designer clothing. You can find a market not only for these things, but just about anything else imaginable.

There are seventy open-air food markets (including three organic markets), each in a different location in the city, open two or three times a week, all year long. Add to this ten covered food markets, and a dozen pedestrian streets where stalls push out on the sidewalk, extending the reach of commerce. We've also included a list of our favorite restaurants. It changes faster than one might imagine, but we have tried to keep up with that fast-moving phenomenon too.

Crisscrossing the city by foot and métro, we visited markets for stamps and phone cards, used books, prints, and fresh flowers. We already knew about the Clignancourt flea market, but got to know the sprawling flea market near the Porte de Vanves, the market for paper items of all kinds just outside the Porte de Vincennes, and many more.

Since completing the initial research ten years ago, much has changed in Paris and in the lives of the writers. This new edition is the result of collaboration between Dixon Long, one of the original authors of this book, and Marjorie Williams, a Boston-based food writer. Together and separately we reviewed all of the markets in the central city, and many farther afield. Much of the text is new, and the shopping suggestions have been updated.

When we go back, we embrace the city as an old friend whose habits and idiosyncrasies we recognize. But it's also a friend who is constantly growing and changing, and who can still surprise, inspire, and enchant us. We've kept our presentations brief, and identified people and places that caught our interest. But you'll make your own discoveries. Whatever your interest or the length of your stay, you'll find a market to fascinate and reward you. So bon voyage, and be sure to visit the markets the next time you see Paris, and the next, and the next . . .

Practical Suggestions

The markets are a great way to see Paris with fresh eyes and to meet the people up close. This guide will take you into parts of the city where you may never have been, and show you markets whose existence you might never have guessed.

The selection of our favorite markets, listed in the first few pages of each arrondissement section, is based on several factors: most are bustling and colorful (such as rue d'Aligre); some are located in places that are interesting for cultural reasons (such as Président Wilson in the elegant 16th arrondissement, and Barbès in the 18th arrondissement, the predominantly North African part of the city). There are also those that offer unusual value or variety, such as the Saint-Germain Arts and Antiques Galleries or the Booksellers on the Seine. Occasional sidebars highlight information that is somewhat tangential, but we found it interesting and thought you might too.

Here are some practical suggestions for making your visits to markets easy, enjoyable, and productive:

✦ Like all great cities of the world, Paris is organized into administrative subdivisions—here they are called arrondissements. They begin with the 1st arrondissement in the heart of the city on the right bank of the Seine and unroll clockwise making two full circles until they end with the 20th arrondissement on the eastern side of the city. Each has a town hall and offers a variety of services not provided by the City of Paris. On street signs, you will see above the street name the number of the arrondissement. Like many guidebooks, *Markets of Paris* is organized by arrondissement.

✦ Always take a map. We like *Paris pratique par arrondissement*, published by l'Indispensable. You can find it in the kiosks on the street, in magazine stands in train stations and bookstores, as a 96-page pocket book, and as a foldout map, Paris Poche. Careful examination will reveal a small blue basket at the site of every open-air food market, and a white basket on a blue background at the sites of the covered markets.

✦ We get around Paris by métro and on foot, using taxis if the weather turns rainy or our feet falter. Friends use the bus, but we find the subway quicker, easier, and drier. We usually buy a *carnet* (a book of ten tickets) because ticket-booths are now rarely available. If there is a long line at the automatic dispensers, look for a *tabac* store with a green sign indicating that they sell métro tickets. For visits longer than a few days, look into the electronic passes (called Navigo) available at most métro stations.

✦ Automated teller machines (ATMs) are generally found inside or near the entrances of banks. Money-changers in small street booths give good service but their rates are somewhat higher. Upscale shops, and some vendors in the larger markets, will take credit cards, but many will not. Most will take a check in euros on a French bank account, if you happen to have one. Bring cash to most markets, preferably in small denominations.

✦ Business hours are not as firm in Paris as in large American cities. The government sets opening and closing hours for the open-air food markets, but you will rarely find much to buy before 8 am, and the stands start to close up by 1 pm. We have listed these practical hours in each case, rather than the official hours. Retail shops generally open at 10 or 11 am and stay open until 6 or 7 pm, but may close for lunch from noon until 2 pm or later. Galleries and antique dealers may open only three or four days a week, from late morning or afternoon to early evening.

✦ In most shops and galleries, travelers can ask that the French value-added tax, or VAT of about 20%, be reimbursed if you spend more than 175 euros in one place. This requires some paperwork, but it's not onerous. You may have to wait in line at the airport for Customs approval, but for large purchases it can be worth the effort.

✦ We're often asked if we bargain: yes, but it helps to be comfortable in French (unless the salesperson speaks English). Prices in food markets are not negotiable, though vendors often lower them dramatically in the last thirty minutes to clear their stands. If you're not sure what price you can get, there's a simple and polite way to ask: "*C'est le meilleur prix?*" (Is that your best price?)

✦ Tipping differs from country to country, and even from region to region within countries. In Paris, a service charge of around 15% is automatically included in the price of a meal. However, if the food or service has been especially satisfactory, there is every reason to leave a small note or some change in the dish that holds the check. When paying for a coffee (and perhaps a croissant) or a glass of wine at a sidewalk café, it's customary to leave a bit more than the amount of the check.

Getting Along in the Food Markets

Making the most of an outing to a Parisian food market cannot be reduced to a simple formula. Go when you're not rushed and take along a sturdy shopping bag, a curious mind, an adventuresome attitude, and a pleasant disposition. Plus cash. (Most merchants don't accept credit cards.) Part of the fun is making discoveries that suit your own interests and appetites. But the first few excursions in any foreign market can be daunting, and the workings of exchange may seem mysterious, so we have distilled some observations from our own experience that might be helpful.

Markets are most vibrant on weekends when they're attended by more people and function both as a shopping excursion and as a social event. On the other hand, less crowded weekdays offer an opportunity to explore the offerings at leisure. You'll know you're in the right vicinity when you see people carrying or rolling heavy shopping bags. Soon you'll spot a cluster of white vans and an array of stalls. Arrive on the early side if you want to avoid crowds and get the best selection, or late if you want the best prices.

Do a lap around the whole market before you decide where to make your purchases. Compare quality and selection. Scope out an *agriculture biologique* stand if organic is important to you. Look for *producteur* signs for items being sold directly by the actual farmers or producers, rather than middlemen. Take note of where lines of customers are waiting since that's a good indicator of some of the best vendors.

Once you've decided where you'd like to buy, look around to see if you need to stand in line. Parisians are accustomed to waiting in queues. For non-Parisians, it isn't always obvious that there even is a line. One reason for the lines is that the locals tend to be loyal to their favorite vendors. Relationships matter a lot. If you have a chance, return to the same vendors for repeated purchases, and you might notice a difference in the way you're treated.

Another behavior worth observing is whether or not customers are selecting the produce themselves. Our habit in America is to handle and inspect items before purchase, but that's often unwelcome in France. Each stand will have its own policy regarding selection. The best advice is to watch other customers and follow their example. If you see baskets within easy reach, that's usually a signal that you are free to choose your own. If you don't see them, wait until you can tell the vendor exactly what you want and how many, one item at a time. They'll do the selection for you. If you spot a bruised or inferior item, speak up politely and ask for a substitute.

It can be helpful to ask what's in season. For best taste, nothing beats fresh local asparagus or green beans or strawberries or melons or cherries—the list is long, but their respective seasons are relatively short. Overflowing piles that you see repeated at many stands (commonly in the center of the display) are often the best indicator, as long as you arrive early. Those items go fastest.

Not only fruits and vegetables follow seasonal cycles. Game meats and certain fowl are generally available only in fall and winter. Same with some outstanding cheeses that make cameo appearances. When buying cheese, tell the vendor when you plan to eat it: today, tomorrow, or in several days makes a difference in their recommendation. It's fun to watch them poke the rinds and expertly pick the perfect ripeness to match your request.

Don't worry if you're not fluent or if your accent is poor. The attempt to express key phrases in French is always appreciated and will make your transactions go more smoothly. Don't fail to greet each vendor with a *Bonjour, Madame* or *Bonjour, Monsieur*. Once the transaction is complete, conclude with a *Merci, au revoir*, and you will receive a polite farewell in return. These basic courtesies are the key to a pleasant experience. One successful encounter fuels the next, and you're ready for another purchase—or another market.

If you have limited time...

Here are the best markets to visit, listed by location, type, name, and page number. Arrondissements are grouped to make it easy to look at a region of Paris rather than one arrondissement at a time.

❖

PARIS CENTER RIGHT BANK (1st, 2nd, 3rd, and 4th *arrondissements*)
Enfants Rouges Covered Market • 50
Rue Montorgueil Market Street • 35
The Flower and Bird Markets • 53
Booksellers on the Seine • 41

❖

PARIS CENTER LEFT BANK (5th, 6th, and 7th *arrondissements*)
Raspail Open-Air Food Market • 73, 81
Rue Mouffetard Market Street • 65
Rue Cler Market Street • 94
Bon Marché Gourmet Food Hall • 89
Left Bank Art and Antiques • 101
Saint-Germain Art and Antiques Galleries • 86
Booksellers on the Seine • 52

❖

PARIS WEST (8th, 16th, and 17th *arrondissements*)
Président Wilson Open-Air Food Market • 215
Batignolles Organic Open-Air Food Market • 105
Postage Stamp and Telephone Card Markets • 111

✦

PARIS NORTH (9th, 10th, 18th, and 19th *arrondissements*)

Barbès Open-Air Food Market • 233

Saint-Quentin Covered Food Market • 137

Galeries Lafayette Gourmet Food Hall • 119

Clignancourt Flea Market • 243

Saint-Pierre Fabric Market • 247

✦

PARIS EAST (11th, 12th, and 20th *arrondissements*)

Bastille Open-Air Food Market • 145

Rue d'Aligre Market Street • 159

Beauvau Covered Food Market • 155

Book and Paper Market • 261

Viaduct Arts and Crafts Shops • 167

✦

PARIS SOUTH (13th, 14th, and 15th *arrondissements*)

Edgar Quinet Open-Air Food Market • 179

Antiquarian and Used Book Market • 211

Edgar Quinet Arts and Crafts Market • 193

Porte de Vanves Flea Market • 195

1st ARRONDISSEMENT • LOUVRE

FOOD MARKETS

Saint-Eustache Les Halles Open-Air Food Market • 24

Saint-Honoré Open-Air Food Market • 25

MARKETPLACES

Louvre of Antiques Dealers • 27

Saint-Honoré Antiques Village • 28

Louvre Underground Shopping Center • 29

Les Halles Underground Shopping Center • 31

Saint-Eustache Les Halles Open-Air Food Market

LE MARCHÉ SAINT-EUSTACHE LES HALLES
Rue Montmartre, between rue Rambuteau and rue du Jour, 1st arr.
🚇 *Châtelet-Les Halles*
Thursday 12:30 pm to 8:30 pm; Sunday 8 am to 2 pm

This small market opened a couple years ago, and although the offerings are relatively limited and their quality uneven, there's the standard market array of fruits and vegetables, cheeses, fish, and prepared foods. Our favorite reason to visit this market is the chance to walk the streets that once formed the heart of Les Halles, the huge central market that dominated central Paris from the 12th century up until the 1960s when it was relocated south of the city to Rungis (see p. 181). The once-beautiful pavilions that housed food stalls have been destroyed, and the city hasn't yet found another way of utilizing the space that satisfies most Parisians. But stroll here and imagine the spectacular world of Les Halles as it was vividly described by Emile Zola in *Le Ventre de Paris* (*The Belly of Paris*): brazen orphans stealing loaves of bread, petulant fishmongers vying for the best location, the greasy stench of sausage-making filling the air. Peek inside the church of Saint-Eustache to find a painted sculpture that depicts the workers of Les Halles and their wagons laden with goods. Several pieces of stained glass are inscribed with symbols of their trades. Only a few other vestiges of this neighborhood's storied past remain, such as the nearby cooking utensils store E. Dehillerin, a pilgrimage destination de rigueur for amateur and professional chefs.

Saint-Honoré Open-Air Food Market

LE MARCHÉ SAINT HONORÉ
Place du Marché Saint-Honoré, 1st arr.
🚇 *Pyramides, Tuileries*
Wednesday 12:30 pm to 8:30 pm; Saturday 8 am to 2 pm

Some Paris markets sprawl over several city blocks and attract large numbers of shoppers from numerous neighborhoods for the vast variety of choices. Others, such as Marché Saint-Honoré, are much smaller and cater to residents or workers in the immediate vicinity, and their desire for items to supplement meals. Don't expect to stumble upon this market, even though it's near place Vendôme and other major sites. This little oasis of a market is tucked off to the side of a large modern glass office building. The mostly pedestrian square is lined with trendy shops and cafés that are popular at lunchtime with the local business crowd. Dedicated merchants are generally cheerful despite the sometimes long lags between customers. For those savvy enough to find this market, the stands offer good fruits, vegetables, cheeses, clothing, and vintage jewelry that can be a welcome respite in between sightseeing the major landmarks of the 1st arrondissement.

Louvre of Antiques Dealers

LE LOUVRE DES ANTIQUAIRES
2, place du Palais Royal, 1st arr.
🚇 *Palais Royal-Musée du Louvre*

This shopping center was closed for renovations, beginning in late 2011 and continuing for twelve to eighteen months. Before closing, two floors of shops were crammed with French decorative artworks and furnishings from the Middle Ages to the twentieth century, as well as a rich mine of material from other times and places. There was no more mesmerizing place in Paris to stroll and, as the French say, *lécher les vitrines* (lick the shop-windows)—even better if you were a serious buyer with money to spend. We expect the renovation will produce an even more impressive collection of authentic wonders from the antique world across the ages and the continents, and will exceed its former achievement.

Saint-Honoré Antiques Village

LE VILLAGE SAINT-HONORÉ

91, rue Saint-Honoré, 1st arr.

🚋 *Louvre-Rivoli*

Tuesday to Sunday 10 am to 6 pm;

some shops close from noon to 2 pm or later

Though it is the smallest of the antiques villages with only ten shops, this collection of dealers is in some respects the most picturesque. It occupies a cul-de-sac in an old and faded part of Paris. These shops offer small vintage objects from the kitchens of yesteryear, and furniture such as wedding mirrors and Provençal dining chairs. A lovely little tearoom with a few outdoor tables makes it worth a look-in, if not a stop for a calming cup of tea.

Louvre Underground Shopping Center

LE CARROUSEL DU LOUVRE
Rue de Rivoli at rue de l'Echelle, 1st arr.
Palais Royal-Musée du Louvre
Tuesday to Sunday 10 am to 6 pm;
some shops are closed from noon until 2 pm or later

This enormous space was excavated beneath the Jardin du Carrousel when the Louvre was renovated some years ago. It's one of the largest indoor shopping spaces in Paris, distinctly and even aggressively modern. Walls and floors of polished marble give a grandiose feeling that depends for its effect not only on height and openness, but also on the quality of construction.

There are a number of fine shops on the main floor, French and foreign, including good places to look for gifts to take home to children and friends. Les Minéraux offers a treasure trove of fascinating minerals and jewelry. For small gifts easy to pack, try L. Appartement. A Virgin Megastore sells CDs, videos, stationery, games, and books.

The invasion of American marketing is evident here, in an Apple store, a Starbucks, and a McDonalds (now common in Paris). But the French luxury vendors still hold their own—leather goods at Le Tanneur, and Pylones for unusual small designer objects. On the way out, take note of Perigot, a shop replete with everything for house-keeping and housecleaning, designed in the most elegant constructions of clear plastic and stainless steel.

Well-organized and efficient restaurants are located on the mezzanine. One has white tablecloths and requires a reservation, if only half an hour ahead. The other is cafeteria-style, but the lines never seem excessively long. The food selection compares favorably with our favorite café in the basement of the gourmet food shop Fauchon.

Le Carrousel has a separate ticket booth and entrance to the Louvre. Sometimes one can avoid the long line of people waiting to enter through the I. M. Pei glass pyramid. There are also meeting rooms, restrooms (not easy to find in the middle of Paris), an underground parking garage, and perhaps best of all, access to the beautifully restored and lighted foundations of the fourteenth-century wall that once surrounded the city. One can sit quietly here, enjoying a cool drink and a sandwich while contemplating these massive and moody subterranean structures.

Les Halles Underground Shopping Center

LE FORUM DES HALLES

*Bounded by rue Rambuteau, rue P. Lescot, rue Berger, and
rue Ballard, 1st arr.*

🚇 *Les Halles, Châtelet*

*10 am to 8 pm every day but Sunday;
restaurants open until 10 pm; cinemas open until 12:30 am*

For 800 years, the area known as Les Halles was a central food-shopping place for Parisians. From about 1500 to the late twentieth century, it grew into an enormous, comprehensive food market. In the 1850s the architect Victor Baltard (see p. 139) designed and oversaw the installation of steel and glass umbrella-style roofs for which he became renowned, and which were copied at other covered markets around the city.

But as Paris expanded and became more crowded, the size and logistical demands of Les Halles became a problem, causing both pedestrian and traffic jams. In the late 1960s, the city decided to move the food market to Rungis near Orly Airport (see p. 181). Once the area was vacated, the congestion cleared up but what remained was a large and unsightly hole in the ground, giving it the nickname *le trou des Halles*—literally, the hole at Les Halles—still more depressing as it lay directly in front of the old and beautiful church of Saint-Eustache.

The city decided to do something. A controversial underground complex of shops, exercise facilities (including an Olympic-size swimming pool), a discothèque, and movie theaters opened in 1979. Visitors now enter a park at ground level, with a large underground shopping mall below, and still deeper, the world's largest underground subway and rail station (including the RER which has lines leading to the suburbs of Paris).

Over time the Forum began to seem unsafe, especially at night. With stores closing, the city of Paris held a competition to renovate the area. In 2007 a design was chosen for a complete overhaul, which continues as of this writing. Above ground the project consists of steel and glass umbrella-like covers over the entrances, evoking the original Les Halles market. The underground space was given a face-lift and some upscale shops were encouraged to locate there (Starbucks among them). Prices are not cheap, and the result is somewhat gloomy and sinister. We do not recommend it except for determined swimmers and the relentlessly curious, like us.

2ND ARRONDISSEMENT • BOURSE

FOOD MARKETS

Rue Montorgueil Market Street • 35

Bourse Open-Air Food Market • 37

Cooking in Paris • 38

MARKETPLACES

Booksellers on the Seine • 41

Covered Passages • 45

Rue Montorgueil Market Street

LA RUE MONTORGUEIL
Rue de Turbigo to rue Réaumur, 2nd arr.

🚊 *Les Halles, Étienne Marcel, Sentier*
Tuesday to Saturday 10 am to 6 pm; Sunday morning

Although it is a heavily touristed area crowded with young people looking for action, there is much to enjoy on this market street. The ambience is shaped by contrasts: modern businesses housed in ancient buildings, pedestrians devouring sandwiches straight out of a bag as they hurry past sidewalk tables filled with leisurely customers, and chic shoppers crisscrossing with occasional beggars.

The street offers a mix of fresh food stalls, restaurants, and other businesses: *charcuteries* and dry cleaners, *boulangeries* and locksmiths, *pâtisseries* and shoe repair shops. If you're staying in the heart of Paris, this will be your market street, and perhaps your restaurant street as well since there are more than twenty of them.

The scale of the buildings is low and regular, giving a feeling of an old, quaint city. But don't be lulled into complacency, because you may need to dodge any number of motorcycles, delivery vans, and bicyclists. Although primarily a pedestrian street, there's plenty of vehicu-

lar traffic to keep strollers alert.

At the rue de Turbigo end of rue Montorgueil, not far from the site of the former great food market at Les Halles, Løv Organic sells eponymous black and herbal teas grown without pesticides. Pâtisserie Stohrer at number 51 sells wonderful chocolate éclairs. Across the street at Poissonnerie Soguisa, men working on slippery tile floors, wearing white aprons and tall rubber boots, help customers select beautiful fresh fish. Nearby at number 78, the restaurant Au Rocher de Cancale is recognizable by its peeling façade and still operates in one of the street's oldest buildings. Once frequented by the writers Honoré de Balzac and Alexandre Dumas, in another era this was the fashionable spot to enjoy oysters after the opera or theater.

We stopped for lunch at the Café du Centre, a pleasant place with brightly colored cane chairs, to sit and people-watch. Directly across the street is Le Palais du Fruit with aisle after aisle of pears, tangerines, apples, mangoes, cherries, and grapes. They also prepare fruit baskets if you're in need of a gift for a local. Another good lunch spot is L'Escargot Montorgueil at number 38, a bistro easily identifiable by the huge golden snail above the door.

Boulangerie Paul has a shop at the corner of Montorgueil and rue Bachaumont. Inside are several tables next to a window where one can eat a sandwich on *pain complet* while watching the baker lean into the oven with a long wooden paddle and pull out a fresh batch of crusty golden baguettes. Another well-known *boulangerie*, Eric Kayser, is located at the top of the market near the intersection with rue Réaumur. Nearby, the window of Maison Collet is filled with pastel meringues, their swirls and peaks rising like waves frozen in a confectionary dance.

Bourse Open-Air Food Market

LE MARCHÉ BOURSE
Place de la Bourse, 2nd arr.
🚇 *Bourse*
Tuesday and Friday 12:30 pm to 8:30 pm

The mayor's office of Paris created several *marchés de l'après-midi*, or afternoon markets, for late-risers and for shoppers who wish to buy a few fresh goods on their way home at the end of the day. Besides Bourse, the other afternoon markets are Anvers, Baudoyer, Bercy, Saint-Eustache, and Saint-Honoré. The Greek columns of the Bourse stock exchange make a classical backdrop for this market, which spreads out on the entrance plaza. Napoleon commissioned the architect Brongniart to design the building after having been pleased with his layout of the Père Lachaise cemetery. We couldn't decide which of the eighteen varieties of salad greens to buy at the vegetable stand, so we picked a bagful of the entire mixture. There's also a fishmonger, *fromagerie*, bookseller, and men selling scarves and African masks. The stands doing the briskest business were ones with food to go—golden paella at one, spicy Creole dishes at another and, most fragrant of all, Polish sausages sizzling in oil with onions that were thinly sliced and arranged on a baguette smeared with Dijon mustard.

COOKING IN PARIS

Visitors to Paris often plan their restaurant itinerary as rigorously as their sightseeing agenda. They literally pack in as much as possible. But eating out all the time gets expensive and, believe it or not, a little tedious. Those who enjoy going to open-air and covered food markets shortchange themselves if all they do is browse. Selecting ingredients and then preparing a meal affords a certain personal pleasure and satisfaction that even an excellent meal at a top restaurant can't match.

One way around the dilemma is to combine the two: learn techniques from a professional chef while doing your own hands-on cooking. With a tip of the toque to Julia Child and others who got their training and inspiration in Paris, cooking classes remain a popular activity.

There are super-serious, diploma-granting programs (think Cordon Bleu and piles of eye-watering onions). At the other extreme, there are half-day workshops offered in home kitchens, bakeries, or restaurants. Even some wine stores are getting in on the action. Search the Internet for options that suit your interest, schedule, and level. Then reserve a spot because slots fill fast.

One version combines a market tour with a cooking class. A guide leads a small group through an outdoor market to buy ingredients and then demonstrates how to whip them into a savory or sweet dish which everyone gets to taste. We found another intriguing option during our last visit when we happened upon 45-minute cooking classes led by professional chefs, and sponsored by the Mayor's office, at occasional outdoor markets. A useful resource for more information about cooking classes is the website of Fédération Française de Cuisine Amateur (FFCA), www.ffcuisineamateur.org.

Let's be clear: Our preference is always "real" food, bought fresh at Parisian markets. But sometimes it's just not possible. On Mondays, for example, markets are closed. In a pinch, one alternative is Picard, a chain of supermarkets that specializes in frozen foods. The flash-freezing method (originated by Charles Birdseye) catches food at the peak of freshness and allows nutrients and flavors to be preserved longer. It has been elevated to an art form by Picard. They sell everything from soup to nuts, literally. Many items have a distinctive French accent—escargots in pastry shells, *béarnaise* and *beurre blanc* sauces, *tarte tatin*. Especially convenient are chopped herbs in frozen cubes, or garlic, shallots, and onions, all minced and ready to go.

Picard stores dot the city. Some are even embedded within market streets. The atmosphere inside is sterile—deep frozen?—like entering a futuristic alternative reality. Several French friends have confessed that they've prepared dinner parties made entirely from Picard—and buried the packaging before guests arrived. Our advice? Open in case of emergency.

Booksellers on the Seine

LES BOUQUINISTES
From quai du Louvre to quai des Célestins, 4th arr.;
from quai Voltaire to quai de la Tournelle, 6th arr.
Tuesday to Friday 2 pm to 6 pm; weekends 11 am to 6 pm;
summer 9:30 am to 7 pm

Booksellers on the Seine came into existence in the mid-sixteenth century. To prevent them from selling forbidden Protestant pamphlets, they were required to have a royal patent. They offered their goods on the Pont Neuf, the first bridge built over the Seine (1606). After the 1789 Revolution, libraries seized from noble families or the clergy ended up for sale on the bridges of Paris.

The ancestors of today's green boxes were wooden trays attached to the bridge parapets with leather straps. In 1891 the *bouquinistes* received permission from the government to hang permanent boxes along the sidewalks bordering the Seine. Each dealer is subject to restrictions regarding the number of boxes (four), the total space occupied (eight meters), and the color of the boxes (dark green). Today the *bouquinistes* are an important resource for collectors of rare botanical prints and early editions. Secondhand books are a mainstay of the trade (the number available is estimated at 300,000), though they are less obvious than magazines, posters, prints, cards, and engravings.

A casual passer-by might take this for a market of the mundane, but closer inspection reveals everything from the commonplace to the arcane, from the titillating to the outrageous. Serious materials shade

off into tourist-oriented trinkets, which is said to provide an increasingly important source of income for vendors. There are currently 250 of them, and one hears that the waiting time to enter the trade is eight years. Business hours of the *bouquinistes* are anything but predictable, though they are supposed to be open at least four days a week. A typical day in the off-season may find half of them open, while a sunny summer day may bring out nearly all.

Whatever the case, they're an established part of the market scene in Paris, and worth an hour's investigation, especially if one has a spe-

cific purpose. We're interested in food and cooking, and found a lot
to look at on the quai de Conti on the Left Bank, opposite the rue de
Guénégaud. Out-of-print cookbooks, old menus, and blank menus for
dinner parties were for sale here. One stand offers a variety of small
plaques (about 4 by 6 inches) called *métals*, with historic advertising
images in full color, of brands such as Coca Cola, Camel cigarettes, Lu
biscuits, and absinthe.

Covered Passages

LES PASSAGES COUVERTS

2nd arrondissement

🚇 *Etienne Marcel, Bourse*

Tuesday to Saturday 10 am to 6 pm, and Sunday morning;
some shops close from noon until 2 pm or later

Covered passages originated in the period after the fall of Napoleon and during the restoration of the House of Bourbon. A new industrial class was emerging, with money to spend and a taste for shopping. At that time the city had no sewers or paved streets, and these narrow, roofed walkways provided an agreeable experience for the wealthy. By the mid-nineteenth century there were more than 150 such passages, many of them near the Palais Royal and within walking distance of the Jardin des Tuileries. Today only eighteen remain. In their heyday, they were elegantly decorated, often covered with glass roofs, offering food and drink, billiards, public baths, and private rooms for carnal pleasures. The arcades, as they are also called in French, began to decline with the arrival of the first modern department store, Au Bon Marché, in 1852.

On a cold, rainy day there is always something to see, buy, eat, or do in the covered passages. Passage du Grand Cerf, not far from the Beaubourg Museum and the Conservatoire des Art et Métiers, connects the rue St. Denis and the rue Dussoubs. Built around 1835, it is the tallest of the passages, at nearly 40 feet enough for three full stories. This passage has a nice sense of style and a bright, airy ambience. Lacy ironwork supports the glass roof, and the simple black and white tile floor gives the

feeling of a Renaissance painting.

Retail shops offer imaginative gift items (Rickshaw), jewelry (Eric and Lydie), and a specialist in aromatherapy featuring fine soaps. Over the years more offices and ateliers have moved in, but there are still some wonderful small specialty shops worth looking into. At the rue St. Denis entrance, a tiny wine bar is quite inviting. At the rue Dussoubs end, you'll find place Goldini, a quiet and restful spot to sit and think for a while.

Another of our favorites for elegance of design and the quality of its shops is Galerie Colbert-Galerie Vivienne. Built in 1823, it connects rue des Petits-Champs, rue Vivienne, and rue de la Banque. A charming tearoom, Priori-Thé, is a good spot to restore the body after a morning on foot. There is also a fine bookshop, to mention only two of several attractions.

These intriguing passages are tucked away in the central city where you may search for them or simply stumble on one. Not all are bright and clean, but almost all have a few surprises.

(For more covered passages, see also 9th arrondissement, p. 127.)

3RD ARRONDISSEMENT · MARAIS

FOOD MARKETS

Enfants Rouges Covered Food Market · 50

Enfants Rouges Covered Food Market

LE MARCHÉ COUVERT ENFANTS ROUGES

39, rue de Bretagne, 3rd arr.

🚇 *Temple, Filles du Calvaire*

Tuesday to Saturday 8:30 am to 1 pm, 4 pm to 7:30 pm;

Friday and Saturday 8:30 am to 8 pm; Sunday 8:30 am to 2 pm

The oldest covered market in Paris, Enfants Rouges was established in 1628 and named for the children dressed in red who were cared for in the orphanage that once occupied the site. The market was closed in the 1980s and the location designated for other uses. An outcry from local residents saved it, but sadly the distinctive Baltard-style building (see p. 139) was destroyed during renovation. Galvanized hoods now protect the stands, and a glass roof keeps out the rain (but not the cold). This reconstructed Enfants Rouges might lack the physical charm of the covered market it replaced, but it is a vibrant and convivial gathering spot. Once inside this tiny paradise in the heart of the Marais, let yourself be carried away by the aromas wafting from the stalls. This market distinguishes itself with its eateries, including Moroccan and Lebanese. Aromas of kabobs and tajines combine with blinis and curries. Buy food to eat later, or place your order and sit at a nearby table where a waiter will serve you.

4TH ARRONDISSEMENT ·
ISLANDS IN THE SEINE

FOOD MARKETS

Baudoyer Open-Air Food Market · 5 2

MARKETPLACES

Booksellers on the Seine · 5 2

The Flower and Bird Markets · 5 3

Saint-Paul Antiques Village · 5 7

Baudoyer Open-Air Food Market

LE MARCHÉ BAUDOYER
Place Baudoyer, 4th arr.
🚇 *Hôtel de Ville*
Wednesday 3 pm to 8 pm; Saturday 8 am to 3 pm

This market sets up a few stands in front of the 4th arrondissement town hall. Alain Balmet has organic breads. In addition, there are stands selling meat, fish, and vegetables, as well as a deli offering ready-to-eat meals such as paella, chicken thighs, and ribs.

Booksellers on the Seine

LES BOUQUINISTES
From quai du Louvre to quai des Célestins, 4th arr.;
from quai Voltaire to quai de la Tournelle, 6th arr.
Tuesday to Friday 2 to 6 pm; weekends 11 am to 6 pm;
summer 9:30 am to 7 pm

You will find a complete description of the Booksellers on p. 41.

The Flower and Bird Markets

LES MARCHÉS AUX FLEURS ET AUX OISEAUX CITÉ
Place Louis Lépine and quai de la Corse,
l'Île de la Cité, 4th arr.

🚇 *Cité*

Flowers: Monday to Saturday 9 am to 6 pm; Birds: Sunday 8 am to 1 pm

Every day but Sunday, the biggest and best flower market in Paris spreads out on the Île de la Cité. On Sunday, the flower shops are closed and the weekly bird market claims the long, open sheds.

Two buildings that look like war relics house specialty shops for orchids, roses, bonsai, and every kind of potted plant, as well as fertilizer, seeds, books, and tools. In the adjacent quai de la Corse, fresh flowers are sold from open stalls by the stem or the bunch. This is the place to come if you want to brighten a rented apartment. Or if you're in a hotel, you may yearn for the color or crave the perfume a bunch of freesias can give.

If you're shopping for small gifts to take home, stop at A.P. Environnement, just opposite the entrance to the Cité métro station. There is an enormous selection of gremlins and griffons, birds and insects, myriad small items to decorate a desk or windowsill or to hide in a small

garden of succulents.

As November 1 comes near (called *Toussaint* or All Saints Day), you'll be staggered by the abundance of chrysanthemums that are traditional for this holiday. In addition, there are many varieties of bamboo, fig, and palm in every season; choisyas, hemlocks, and heathers compound the blend and add to the charm. Whatever the reason or season, a stroll through this extraordinary market is a delight to one's senses, a calm and refreshing stop amid the clamor and bustle of Paris. Au Jardin d'Edgar features miniature plants, including bonsai, for terraces and balconies. Take a look at La Maison de l'Orchidée et Plantes Carnivores/Sensitives for something truly different. Claude Bouchard sells dolls known as Santons de Provence in historic costumes, and tea towels with regional themes in case your trip doesn't include time in the south.

On Sunday, perhaps not every bird imaginable as a pet can be found here, but you'll see everything that thrives in the Parisian climate. In the largest cages are solemn grey parrots, and beside them their green cousins, raucous as clowns, nudging and crowding each other on their perches like naughty boys. The market resonates with their trills and whistles, and occasionally a wild screech knifes through the air. Established sellers are arrayed against the backs of the sheds with their big birds, fat sacks of seed, and elaborate cages. Their merchandise is protected from wind and weather, and clients can be comfortable in all but the most inclement conditions. Along the sidewalk under the edge of the roof are vendors with stacks of small cages holding dazzling little multicolored finches and delightful golden canaries.

There is equipment for raising and keeping birds, cages of every size and style, bird medicines, and books about the classification and

care of songbirds. Charming outdoor birdhouses are for sale, and in the same stall as many as fifty different kinds of birdseed. Down the center of the market is the casual trade, people with a few nestlings or a single bird. There are scruffy interlopers here too: a rough-looking fellow with a basin of goldfish and a box of turtles; a mysterious gypsy woman who sometimes shows up with a basket of puppies. In the spring, bunnies are displayed. Children stroke their fur and dream of taking one home. Around Easter time there are little chicks to make a child smile.

Saint-Paul Antiques Village

LE VILLAGE SAINT-PAUL

Rue Saint-Paul, near the corner of rue Charlemagne, 4th arr.

🚇 *Saint-Paul*

Tuesday to Sunday 10 am to 12 pm, 2 pm to 6 pm;
some shops may open later

About thirty small shops are housed in renovated residential buildings on the right bank of the Seine, behind the church of Saint-Paul and Saint-Louis. Enter on rue Charlemagne, where you will be guided to the center of this little village by small flags announcing Village Saint-Paul. The setting of this little village is rather severe, but the inner courtyards, paved with large granite bricks, are quiet and pleasant, with interesting shops: Cassiopée for silver and porcelain; Aquamarin for jewelry; Des Photographes where you can find old books, prints, and cards; and antiques at Monde Secret. Fable du Logis sells glass and ceramics, and a small café called Cru Barallin specializes in fish and meats, both cooked and raw.

On the rue Saint-Paul, La Célestine has studio ceramics. Across the street toward rue Saint-Antoine is a lovely little English language bookshop, The Red Wheelbarrow, founded and run by a Canadian. You can find here all the latest books about Paris and its thousand and one delights.

5TH ARRONDISSEMENT ✦ LATIN QUARTER

FOOD MARKETS

Place Monge Open-Air Food Market • 6 1

Rue Mouffetard Market Street • 6 5

Maubert Open-Air Food Market • 6 9

Port Royal Open-Air Food Market • 7 0

MARKETPLACES

Booksellers on the Seine • 7 0

Place Monge Open-Air Food Market

LE MARCHÉ MONGE

Place Monge, 5th arr.

🚇 *Monge*

Wednesday and Friday 8 am to 1:30 pm; Sunday 8 am to 2 pm

Marché Monge occupies a charming square in the heart of the Left Bank directly above a métro stop and quite near rue Mouffetard. Many Parisians claim it as their favorite. White vans park bumper-to-bumper around the periphery on market days, their disgorged goods crafted into attractive displays. At the crest of one slight hill and the base of another, place Monge has the perfect dimensions for an open-air market: small enough to feel intimate, yet large enough to host forty vendors and a crowd of shoppers during peak hours. Young plane trees with protective iron aprons around their bases poke up from the asphalt and provide welcome shade during the warm season.

A circular fountain splashes at the center of the square, casting a gentle spell. Children play around its edges while pigeons watch from atop vintage lampposts. There's nothing pretentious about this market. A good spirit flows as freely as the water feature. Friendly merchants sometimes offer samples to taste. They greet families, couples, and singles who patiently wait in line and carry bags laden with purchases.

Mounds of fresh produce, quality meats, fish, cheeses, olives, nuts, and dried fruits catch the eye and tempt the appetite. Several stalls specialize in *agriculture biologique* (organic) produce. Others such as Les Vergers de la Terre Saine sell crisp pears and apples in various shapes

and hues picked from orchards in the Picardie region. There's a good selection of salad greens. At P. Casson, the heads of lettuce go fast. By noon all that's left of them is a scattering of torn leaves. Across the aisle a *charcuterie* sells hearty *choucroute* made of hot sauerkraut, white wine, and smoked bacon. A line forms at Tan Sir Ti for good-quality, reasonably priced fruits and vegetables. Cheeses pile high at La Petite Fermière Leitao where the selection is hardly dented as customers make their choices. We can't resist a ripe round of ash-coated goat cheese. Gilles LeGall brings bins of oysters and other sea-farmed shellfish straight from Brittany. Directly across from fishmonger Chez Loulou is another special find—the potatoes and carrots grown by Monsieur Léo

Zamba, who will also explain how best to prepare them.

It would be easy to mistake this market for a world's fair given its range of ethnic cuisines. A Lebanese man offers a taste of pita smeared with creamy yogurt. The aroma of curry rises where a native North African heats her culinary specialties. Equally enterprising, a young French woman puts her art school training to use with beautifully crafted *financiers*, or teacakes, flavored with ginger, orchid, and pistachio. Toward the edges of this bustling market, the goods shift to non-edible items that are tempting in their own way—scarves and jewelry, clothing, carpets, and African statues and masks.

Rue Mouffetard Market Street

LA RUE MOUFFETARD

Rue Calvin to rue Edouard Quénu/rue Censier, 5th arr.

🚇 *Place Monge, Censier Daubenton*

Tuesday to Saturday 10 am to 6 pm; Sunday morning

Some people say they're not really back in Paris until they're on rue Mouffetard. This picturesque market stretches up and down a well-worn cobblestone street with a distinctive medieval character. The church of Saint-Geneviève lies on the south side of Mont Saint-Geneviève, named for the patron saint of Paris. Old buildings, some with bulging timbers, press into the narrow street and enhance this market's charm. Lift your eyes to take in the signs and flourishes above some doorways, even as the temptations at street level entice. Above number 69 is a carving from the masthead of a sunken ship. The sign above number 122 depicts two boys, dressed in the style of Henry IV's reign, drawing water from a well. Extravagantly decorated panels adorn the façade at number 134.

Scholars date the market's origins to 1350, although official records begin in 1654. Lurid events occurred here. In the 1700s, for example, the burial ground of a young Jansenist priest attracted girls who expressed their religious ecstasy by falling into hysteria and self-flagellation. Today, the street is one of Paris's most popular and is often crowded with tourists. A colorful procession of shoppers and gawkers weaves up and down the gently sloping hill. At the uphill end by place de la Contrescarpe, several cafés cluster around a central fountain. Café Delmas, on the south-facing side, is crowded when sunshine is the priority.

Across the square, La Contrescarpe is nicely shaded and busy in its turn. Numerous *crêperies* and restaurants specialize in *fondue* and *raclette*. Downhill a little farther, Au Petit Bistro and Café Le Mouffetard offer a classic setting and dependable dishes.

Food stalls cluster at the lower end of this ancient street. Numerous excellent *fromageries*, *boucheries*, *boulangeries*, and *poissonneries* attract lines of shoppers. Le Fournil de Mouffetard sells outstanding breads and pastries. The rotisserie chicken at Boucherie Saint-Médard tempts us for a ready-made dinner. Pomi V's stands of fresh produce permit self-service, which makes shopping fast and efficient. Perfect pyramids of oranges and apples are demolished by determined shoppers as noon approaches. The Italian delicatessen Delizius and cheese shop Androuet share the storefront under ornate wooden panels depicting boars, deer, and bucolic rural scenes. Several well-known stores have taken root here too, such as Olivier & Co. and L'Occitane; Picard has recently installed a selection of frozen items.

At the base of the hill and near a twelfth-century church, the market spills onto square Saint-Médard. An accordion player, cabaret-style singers, and costumed dancers add gaiety to this quintessential Parisian market and even distribute song sheets for sing-alongs. When you emerge at this end of the street, few things could be more appealing than half an hour's respite with a glass of wine or a *pastis* at Cave la Bourgogne with its pleasant outlook on the corner of rue Edouard Quénu.

Maubert Open-Air Food Market

LE MARCHÉ MAUBERT-MUTUALITÉ

Place Maubert, 5th arr.

🚊 *Maubert-Mutualit*

Tuesday, Thursday, and Saturday 8 am to 1:30 pm

The city's oldest known market—Palu—began in the fifth century on l'Île de la Cité, when Paris was called Lutetia. By 1547, Palu had outgrown the space. It was moved to its present site on boulevard Saint-Germain and renamed Marché Maubert. Then, as now, it attracted travelers, academics associated with the Sorbonne, and neighborhood residents. Though smaller than the nearby market in place Monge, this one is energetic and eclectic. It includes a large stand selling organic produce. Established shops in the little square near the métro, such as the outstanding Laurent Dubois for cheeses, round out the offerings.

Port Royal Open-Air Food Market

LE MARCHÉ PORT ROYAL

Boulevard de Port Royal, in front of the Hôpital du Val de Grâce, 5th arr.

🚇 *Port-Royal*

Tuesday, Thursday, and Saturday 8 am to 1 pm

Port Royal occupies a stretch of sidewalk on the south side of the Val de Grâce hospital, an extraordinarily beautiful building in a large and gracious park. This small neighborhood market has the customary array of meat, fish, fowl, and produce stands, and some inexpensive clothing. Here as in le Marché Monge, Gilles LeGall sells sea-farmed oysters and mussels from Brittany.

Booksellers on the Seine

LES BOUQUINISTES

From quai du Louvre to quai des Célestins, 4th arr.;
from quai Voltaire to quai de la Tournelle, 6th arr.
Tuesday to Friday 2 to 6 pm; weekends 11 am to 6 pm;
summer 9:30 am to 7 pm

You will find a complete description of the Booksellers on p. 41.

6TH ARRONDISSEMENT · SAINT-GERMAIN

FOOD MARKETS

Raspail Open-Air Food Market · 73

Artisan Bakers and Artisan Foods · 77

Raspail Organic Open-Air Food Market · 81

Saint-Germain Covered Food Market · 85

MARKETPLACES

Booksellers on the Seine · 86

Saint-Germain Art and Antiques Galleries · 86

Raspail Open-Air Food Market

LE MARCHÉ RASPAIL

Boulevard Raspail from rue du Cherche-Midi to rue de Rennes, 6th arr.

🚇 *Rennes*

Tuesday and Friday 8 am to 1:30 pm; Sunday 8 am to 3 pm

(for the Raspail Organic Food Market, see p. 81)

Boulevard Raspail cuts through the 6th arrondissement from the boulevard Saint-Germain to place Denfert-Rochereau, sloping gently upward as it goes south, intersecting several métro and bus stops en route. The ease of getting around makes Marché Raspail a reasonable alternative for shoppers coming from other neighborhoods. Some arrive with fur coats, others in ragged jeans. London plane trees dot the boulevard, and large circular plantings in the median strip break up the monotony of a straight line. This partly explains the pleasant atmosphere, but it's

enhanced by friendly vendors and their overflowing horn of plenty. All combined, it's a cinch to enjoy this market and completely zone out the cars, motorcycles, and trucks that rumble past on both sides.

In the early 1900s, a movement to disband covered markets led to the creation of this open-air food market, along with those at Place Monge, Port-Royal, and Télégraphe. Vegetables and fruits dominate (at least nine stalls), but there's also an excellent selection of fish, meats, and cheeses. For appetites that lean toward non-food items, there's also plenty from which to choose: cashmere sweaters, scarves, straw hats, baskets, and housewares. On one visit, our second market of the day, our tired legs ached to sit in the chairs assembled off to a side—until we noticed that the seats or wicker backs were missing. A young man

explained that he attracts customers at these markets for his furniture repair and re-upholstery business. He offers to pick-up and deliver, but not to rent!

We were revived after tasting slices of baguette spread with duck and goose foie gras offered by Monsieur Grémillet at Lafitte. He extended a well-worn cutting board covered with samples, encouraging us to compare the flavors. Goose was creamier, and he explained that it's harder to breed geese, which accounts for the 40% higher price. His wife runs the Lafitte family operation, now in its sixth generation. He advised anyone taking foie gras outside France to buy vacuum-packed tins instead of glass jars. The very affable monsieur was as willing to discuss politics as he was foie gras.

Many of the produce vendors procure their goods at Rungis, but several are the actual growers who sell direct. Daniel Noé, for example, brings seasonal vegetables grown in his garden in Montlhéry not far outside Paris: fat moons of salad greens, cabbage with leaves curling like velvety green dresses, and cooked red beets ready to slide out of their skins at a touch. For a selection of choice nuts, olives, oil-cured tomatoes, and homemade tapenades, Maison Nouri can't be missed. We buy pâté made from rabbit at the most pristine of the charcuterie stands simply because we've never tried it before, and then supplement it with fresh julienned carrot salad and *feuillantine provençale* (small pizza-like rounds topped with sun-dried tomatoes and cheese).

We ask two different vendors how the open-air markets are doing in the face of competition from the supermarkets. A cheese maker frets that he has noticed a drop in business. The quality of his *fromage* and other dairy items far exceed what can be bought in supermarkets, but he can't match their prices. A few stalls down, a man selling dried herb mixtures voices a more optimistic opinion. Business dropped during the financial crisis, he admits, but he believes supermarkets are turning off shoppers, who are beginning to value the experience and quality offered by small local markets. The jury is out, but we hope he's right.

ARTISAN BAKERS AND ARTISAN FOODS

One of the best things to eat in Paris—or anywhere in France, for that matter—is bread. A new generation of bakers is turning up the heat on the country's best-loved carb, churning out traditional baguettes and multigrain loaves, thin *ficelles* (literally "strings") and hefty round *boules*, in varieties that are nutted, seeded, fruited, organic, and gluten-free. Paris now hosts the Coupe du Monde de la Boulangerie (the Olympics of Baking) where international teams compete and help keep bread-baking standards high.

Poilâne is among Paris's oldest and most famous bakeries. The original shop in the heart of Saint-Germain-des-Prés has baked bread the same way since it was opened by Pierre Poilâne in 1932. This bread is made with slow-rising, natural yeast, baked in a wood-fired oven.

The sourdough starter gives it a distinctively rustic flavor. A cursive "P" adorns each signature loaf. Pierre Poilâne passed the business to his son Lionel, who died tragically in a helicopter accident in 2002. Since then, his daughter Apollonia has run the bakery in the family tradition. (Poilâne Bakery, 8, rue du Cherche-Midi, 6th arrondissement, Monday to Saturday, 7:15 am to 8:15 pm. Also at 38, rue Debelleyeme, 3rd arrondissement, Tuesday to Sunday, same hours.)

A stop at this delightful shop can include a visit to the oven in the basement, a wood-fired giant that is partly responsible for the special quality of the product. We went down a winding stone staircase, its treads hollowed by years of use. In a vaulted and insufferably hot cellar of smooth, brown limestone, one man was working alone in shorts and heavy shoes, stoking the fire, pulling baked goods in and out of the oven with the rhythm of long experience. Like all traditional bakers, he used a thin, flat paddle at the end of a ten-foot long handle to put loaves of bread or sheets of cookies into the oven and locate them for the best exposure to the heat. His eight-hour shift alternates with other bakers, so the oven is going around the clock.

We were offered a taste of oven-fresh Punitions, the nickname (meaning "punishments") given to Poilâne's butter cookies that have a loyal following all over the world. The story goes that Pierre's grandmother in Normandy would call the children, seemingly to punish them, but instead pull from her apron a handful of butter cookies. Punitions are not too sweet, but crisp with a hint of cinnamon.

Big baskets of rising bread dough were stacked on racks along the walls, waiting their turn in the oven. The baker pinched off a bit so we could savor the yeasty, sour flavor for which Poilâne is justly famous.

The first loaves were ready to come out of the oven. The baker lifted them one by one on his paddle and stacked them in a rack. Their aroma flooded the room, triggering a basic instinct, and we raced upstairs to get in line for our loaf.

The popular revival of artisan methods for bread baking, led by innovators such as Poilâne, is creating similar ripples in other food categories. It's common now to see "artisan" in signs for bakers, butchers, brewers, cheese shops, *chocolatiers*—even ice cream. What does it mean? The cynical response is that it's a marketing buzzword for "expect to pay more." But we dug deeper (not just in our pockets) to understand.

Artisan foods are produced by traditional, non-industrial methods. They're made in labor-intensive small batches and usually from the best ingredients, sourced locally. The methods are those that used to be handed down through generations, but over the years were threatened with being lost or forgotten due to reliance on industrialized processes. The artisan label usually applies to foods that involve fermentation (bread, cheese, beer, dairy, *charcuterie*) where the slower, natural methods allow flavors to develop to their fullest. Flavor is the point. Artisan producers know where their raw materials come from and understand the implications for taste—all of which is bound up in what the French call *terroir*. You may pay more, but in our experience it's generally worth it.

Raspail Organic Open-Air Food Market

LE MARCHÉ BIOLOGIQUE RASPAIL

Boulevard Raspail from rue du Cherche-Midi to rue de Rennes, 6th arr.

🚆 *Rennes*

Sunday 9 am to 3 pm

(for the Raspail regular food market on Tuesdays and Fridays, see p. 73)

At one time a fringe offshoot of the regular Raspail market, this Sunday market has fully come into its own. It attracts a large and loyal clientele, many of whom travel far to shop here. One of the biggest changes in the Paris market scene in recent years has been the spike of interest in organic. The Raspail Sunday market is one of three organic markets in the city, and certainly the largest and most widely known. Often it's referred to in the singular as "Le Marché Bio," and many claim it's the crème de la crème of all Paris's markets—for those who can afford it.

It's located in the same spot as the regular weekday version of the Raspail market (starting a bit south of Hôtel Lutétia, with its grand art deco façade); however, the merchants and customers who turn up on Sunday tend to be different. They are often passionate about their commitment to organic but don't talk much about it—mostly because business is brisk, and there usually isn't time for relaxed conversation.

C'Bio is one of several excellent vendors of seasonal fruits and vegetables. Provibio is another of our favorites. Sales people will point out the freshest seasonal options, if asked. The meats sold at this market come from animals that were raised in better than average conditions. There's also an abundance of small-boat, line-caught fish. Cheesemongers at the *bio* markets sell fewer varieties because of the stricter requirements for organic dairy, but the options are just as delicious. Bread and pastry sellers abound too. Le Pain du Midi offers whole-grain, nut, and seeded breads. English muffins and other baked goods at Valérie Debiais-Healey's stand have garnered acclaim. Her husband, from New Jersey, came up with the recipes. Another of our regular stops is La Cucina for fresh pasta, antipasti, and other Italian specialties. The cheerful staff, adorned in hats and striped shirts, often look as if they just stepped off gondolas along the Seine.

This market is as much about stocking up for later as it is about instant gratification. Several tantalizing specialties are made on the premises and consumed there too. A large skillet of simmering paella can be found at Interface 3000—just let your nose lead you to it. At Buvette du Marché, near the middle of the market, a man pours freshly made hot chocolate, chai, and mint tea. Toward the rue du Cherche-Midi end of the market, potato-onion pancakes sizzle on the griddle at the always-popular Les Gallatins stand. Don't even bother trying to muster the willpower to save them for later. They're best hot and fresh, with a twang of cheesy flavor. If you buy extra, they can be reheated in a skillet.

Most of the non-edible goods reflect the spirit of environmental consciousness: biodegradable detergents and soaps, essential oils, herbal remedies, organic beauty products, cotton clothing, non-coated cookware, etc. But it's the food that's the main draw. A favorite among foodies, organic enthusiasts, and other locals who enjoy this lively Sunday scene, the Raspail *bio* market has also become a major draw for tourists.

Crowds typically fill the sidewalk by late morning, but a pleasant atmosphere and convivial mood still prevail.

Saint-Germain Covered Food Market

LE MARCHÉ COUVERT SAINT-GERMAIN-DES-PRÉS
4-6, rue Lobineau, 6th arr.
🚇 *Odéon, Mabillon*
Tuesday to Saturday 8:30 am to 1 pm, 4 pm to 7:30 pm;
Sunday 8 am to 1 pm; clothing shops are open from 10 am to 7:30 pm

During the Middle Ages, this was the site of the celebrated Saint-Germain Fair, where monks from the nearby church hosted a popular arts and trades gathering. Subsequently a historic covered market, most traces of its past are now gone. In 1813, it became a popular covered market in a Parthenon-inspired building. A bland renovation in 1992, designed to accommodate upscale clothing shops, eradicated most vestiges of the site's illustrious history. Fortunately, part of the ground floor was preserved as a food market. The produce is fresh and nicely displayed in a calm and pleasant atmosphere compared with the tumult of the typical Parisian market. Prices are somewhat high, but on a rainy day in the heart of the Left Bank, that may be less important than keeping dry. Several excellent vendors offer a good selection and make a visit worthwhile. J'Go Les Jardins occupies the large space in the center and represents producers from southwestern France who are identified on small blackboards. The emphasis is on fresh, seasonal items. Also of note, the wine shop Bacchus and Ariane, and the fish market La Caravelle. In the northwest corner of the building you'll find a welcoming Irish pub called Coolin (not pronounced the French way, but the Irish).

Booksellers on the Seine

LES BOUQUINISTES
from quai Voltaire to quai de la Tournelle, 6th arr.
Tuesday to Friday 2 to 6 pm;
weekends 11 am to 6 pm; summer 9:30 am to 7 pm

You will find a complete description of the Booksellers on p. 41.

Saint-Germain Art and Antiques Galleries

LE CARRÉ DES ARTS SAINT-GERMAIN
Between the quai Malaquais-quai Conti-quai des Grands Augustins,
boulevard Saint-Germain, and rue des Saints-Pères, 6th arr.
🚇 *Saint-Michel, Cluny-la-Sorbonne, Odéon*
Daily except Monday 10 am to 6 pm;
some shops close from noon to 2 pm or later

This collection of more than one hundred galleries and shops, not unlike the Carré des Antiquaires, is an association that sponsors events to focus attention on their location and diversity as purveyors of fine art. One can wander for a long time in narrow streets that are home to every kind of antique, art and craft shop. Sellers specializing in home decoration can also be found here. At any given time, a few galleries will have shows in progress that you are welcome to visit. Don't hesitate to go in, say *bonjour*, and look around.

7TH ARRONDISSEMENT • EIFFEL TOWER

FOOD MARKETS

Bon Marché Gourmet Food Hall • 89

About Oysters • 92

Rue Cler Market Street • 94

Saxe-Breteuil Open-Air Food Market • 97

MARKETPLACES

Left Bank Art and Antiques • 101

Swiss Village Antiques • 102

F
77.177.01
CEE
Saint Nectaire fermier
AOP
17.80 euros
ROQUEFORT
Depuis 1906
PAPILLON
Affinage en Caves Naturelles
ROQUEFORT
Depuis 1906
PAPILLON
Affinage en Caves Naturelles
1906
PAPILLON

Bon Marché Gourmet Food Hall

LA GRANDE ÉPICERIE AU BON MARCHÉ
Rue de Sèvres at rue du Bac, 7th arr.
🚇 *Sèvres-Babylone*
Monday to Saturday 8:30 am to 9 pm
(main store: Monday, Tuesday, Wednesday, and
Saturday 10 am to 8 pm; Thursday and Friday 10 am to 9 pm)

La Grande Épicerie might be the best gourmet food market in the city, if not one of the best in the world. It offers even the most sophisticated of palates a huge array of delicacies, wines, beers, and sumptuous prepared foods. This food emporium occupies the building directly across the street from its parent, the Bon Marché department store. The merchandiser's knack for creating eye-catching displays is put to good use. Beautiful presentations, bright lighting, and broad aisles make us wide-eyed—and eager to keep piling items into our cart. But of course the temptations come at a price. This is one of the most expensive food shops in Paris.

Three full aisles are dedicated to biscuits alone, while nearby aisles are devoted to salt (including an impressive selection of *sel de mer*, or sea salt), teas, jams, and bonbons. Enough confections to make a dentist tremble come in colorful collectible containers. Others, sold by weight, gleam in glass jars. Several high-end brands get prized real estate of their own, such as Hediard, Maxim's, and Fortnum and Mason. Some aisles are devoted to foods popular in other countries (although why the Grande Bretagne display includes all-American Hellmann's may-

onnaise and Campbell's soup seems odd). The United States section includes peanut butter, marshmallows, bottled barbeque sauces, and other packaged goods. Elsewhere, the internationally sourced goods are shelved together. One of the dairy cases, for example, gives Philadelphia cream cheese equal billing alongside Longley Farm (U.K.) extra rich Jersey cream, and Isigny Sainte-Mère (Normandy) *crème fraîche*.

Almost any preserved food you can think of in a box or a can is somewhere on these shelves. Plus there's an equally impressive array of fresh foods. Racks of vegetables and fruits submit to gentle sprays of moisture like a fancy spa treatment. Artfully decorated fruit tarts and chocolate cakes are prepared on premises. Fresh-baked breads are stacked vertically and horizontally on shelves like an edible tic-tac-toe game. Fish practically swim atop the white surf of ice. The cheeses,

meats, and *charcuterie* are just as dazzling.

If you get hungry—or simply need a break to clear your head—there's seating off to the side called Le PicNic where customers perch on stools at shared tables. The second floor has been refurbished with a chic Italian café called Primo Piano and a garden that's open to the sky. La Grande Épicerie is a pleasing place to find food-related gifts. Another option is to buy a box from the front desk and assemble your own assortment, which they will then wrap (but not ship). Whatever you buy, the quality will be high but so too the tab. And yet the experience of getting lost in the seemingly endless aisles of tantalizing food is itself worth an afternoon's entertainment.

ABOUT OYSTERS

We believe that nowhere in the world are more oysters consumed per person than in Paris. Some data support this position, though it would be hard to prove. Nevertheless, by our definition of a market as a place where you can find a lot of the same kind of thing at competitive prices, it would seem that Paris is a virtual marketplace for oysters, at least from September 1 to May 15.

First to note is that oysters are widely available at the brasseries, cafés, and restaurants around the city and in the open markets. We are confident that they are fresh, having been rushed from the Atlantic coast (Normandy, Brittany, Arcachon Bay) and the Mediterranean by truck.

Second to note is the difference between two main types of oyster: *plate* or flat, and *creuse* or curved/crenellated. The flats are commonly called *belons*; they come from Brittany, where only about 1,500 tons a year are produced, of 130,000 tons of all oysters harvested. The most common and most popular *creuse* are called *fines de claires*; they are raised in ponds in Marennes-Oléron. *Fines de claires* are numbered from 0 to distinguish the largest (150 grams or more) to 5, the smallest (30 to 40 grams).

Only the flat oyster was produced in French waters until 1868, when a Portuguese vessel laden with oysters was trapped in the Gironde estuary by a storm. Thinking his cargo was spoiled, the captain ordered the whole lot dumped overboard. They thrived and became known as *Portugaises*. In the 1970s a disease wiped out nearly the entire population, resulting in the introduction of a hardy and disease-resistant oyster from Japan. The *Japonaise*, practically indistinguishable from the *Portugaise*, is now the main type of *creuse* found in the market.

Charles de Gaulle's famous remark about the difficulty of governing a country that produces 300 cheeses could as easily have been made about oysters, of which there are some 246 different kinds. True aficionados claim to have one or more favorites. Personally, we prefer the *belons*, which to us have greater delicacy and more of the flavor of the sea. But when it comes to oysters, to each his or her own.

Rue Cler Market Street

LA RUE CLER

Rue de Grenelle to avenue de la Motte Picquet, 7th arr.

🚉 *École Militaire*

Tuesday to Saturday 10 am to 6 pm; Sunday morning

This bright and cheerful market street is surely one of the most pleasant in all of Paris. Rue Cler's wide and welcoming pedestrian walkway cuts through an upscale neighborhood that's near several major tourist attractions—Tour Eiffel, Hôtel des Invalides, and École Militaire. But it's a favorite of locals as well as tourists. Its attraction lies in the uniformly high quality of items found here as well as the ample choice of

cafés interspersed among the shops, which makes it a convenient spot for meeting friends.

Davoli draws a large and loyal clientele for its exceptional Italian specialties and prepared foods, both hot and cold. Previously known as La Maison du Jambon, the name was changed to avoid confusion with orders that were being delivered to another store by that name. A box of Pralina con Tartufo, or truffle pralines, makes a great treat —or gift, depending on your willpower. Stéphane Davoli, a great-grandson of the founder, takes pride in the fact that they still import their provisions from the family's native Reggio-Emilia region in Italy. A woman next to us swooned over her choice of hot ravioli stuffed with mushrooms, and insisted that next time we try the smoked salmon.

A couple of doors down, the flowers at Floralies invoke springtime even on a grey and chilly February day. We bought bunches of yellow tulips and purple freesia. The salesgirl grabbed a few extra pieces of greenery to include with the purchase and tied them together with a pretty straw bow.

Amorino sells homemade ice cream without artificial coloring or flavors, made with *bio* (organic) eggs and milk. Although the company was founded in Milan, the ice creams sold here are made in Paris, and this is one of several shops. Across the street, the windows of La Mère de la Famille remind us that Valentine's Day is approaching, with attractively displayed boxes of fine chocolates alternately stamped *Je t'aime un peu, beaucoup, à la folie, et passionnément* (I love you a little, a lot, madly, and passionately).

Off rue Cler a few doors down on rue du Champ de Mars, L'Épicerie Fine is worth a short side trip. They sell spices from all over the world along with French mustards, *fleur de sel*, and half-pints of the world-famous Berthillon ice cream. Tall jars of dry beans, including the large white *tarbais* variety, which are great for making cassoulet, can be found here too. The shopkeeper observed that younger people in France are experimenting with spices far more than previous generations.

Saxe-Breteuil Open-Air Food Market

LE MARCHÉ SAXE-BRETEUIL

Avenue de Saxe from place de Breteuil to avenue de Ségur, 7th arr.

🚇 *Ségur, Duroc*

Thursday 8 am to 1:30 pm; Saturday 8 am to 2 pm

The intersection of several grand avenues anchors this market and makes for some impressive sight lines. The Eiffel Tower rises not far away in a view that's perfectly framed by the tree-lined avenue de Saxe. It almost appears as if the market is a large picnic spread at the feet of the famous tower. Looking northward along avenue de Breteuil, the majestic gold-domed Invalides, which houses Napoleon's tomb, reflects the morning sun. Turn in the other direction, and Montparnasse Tower juts skyward in the distance. A statue of Louis Pasteur stands guard in the hub of place de Breteuil rotary. His austere gaze traverses the well-manicured lawns and luxurious apartment buildings that characterize this neighborhood.

Marché Saxe-Breteuil draws an elegant crowd, and even the dogs are well coiffed. When the King's court left the Louvre in the 1600s, many of the nobility resettled in this area for its convenience to the King's new home in Versailles as well as the large tracts of attractive land. To this day, the neighborhood maintains an aura of privilege and prestige. A tranquil mood pervades. The polite chatter of friendly transactions mixes with the hushed baritone of church bells tolling noontime.

Two parallel aisles of stalls host a variety of vendors. Their goods are shaded by canvas awnings and the dappled canopy of sycamores.

Behind one of the vegetable stands, Monique Quillet, also known as the singing salad lady, chirps a lovely tune while weighing customers' orders. She performs in local cabarets during her off-hours. Several producers bring items directly from their own land, including apples and pears, verdant salad greens, and wines. Pig's trotters and assorted animals' tongues, kidneys, hearts, and testicles are on vivid display as delicacies at the *triperie*. Friendly fishmongers and cheese-makers share gossip with regular customers. We buy fresh pasta at Daga for dinner and then, for immediate gratification, pick up samosas and curried North African specialties for a picnic lunch on the benches that line the nearby green esplanade.

In addition to the usual complement of food stalls, there's a wide

choice of clothing. It ranges from sequined cocktail dresses and fur coats to cotton pajamas and summer shirts. We concealed our surprise when a woman stripped down to her underwear without any evident self-consciousness to try on a pair of linen trousers. Madame Attal sells feathery hats, and a tourist snaps up one in fuchsia. Other stands sell a variety of household items, jewelry, tablecloths, carpets, and leather goods known as *maroquinerie* (because they come from Morocco). On the edge of the market, we couldn't resist a bunch of sweet-smelling lilacs wrapped in newspaper that was extended to all passers-by. We told the woman to keep the extra euro of change. She gratefully accepted, then handed us a second big bunch for free.

Left Bank Art and Antiques

LE CARRÉ RIVE GAUCHE

*In the area bounded by the quai Voltaire, rue de l'Université,
rue des Saints-Pères, and rue du Bac
(internal streets are rue de Beaune, rue de Verneuil, and rue Allent), 7th arr.
🚇 Musée d'Orsay, Solférino
Monday to Saturday 10 am to 6 pm;
some shops close from noon to 2 pm or later*

More than one hundred upscale shops in the area behind the Musée d'Orsay offer all kinds of antiques (furniture, porcelain, glass, sculpture, painting, rugs, tapestries) from around the world. Most shops belong to a neighborhood association and display a flag about the size of a briefcase over their doors. It changes from year to year—in 2011 it

was composed of six rectangles of different sizes in black, dark blue, and light blue. Many years ago we bought Oriental carpets at Galerie Diurne, and still enjoy them. The concentration of dealers here is fully as impressive as the collection across the river in the Louvre des Antiquaires. It will surely become more important because the Louvre des Antiquaires has closed for renovations (see p. 27).

Swiss Village Antiques

LE VILLAGE SUISSE
Avenue de Suffren, between rue Dupleix and
avenue de la Motte Piquet, 7th arr.
🚇 *La Motte Piquet-Grenelle*
Thursday to Monday 10 am to 7 pm;
some shops close from noon to 2 pm or later

A sign tells us that this market was established in 1900, but the buildings that house it look more like they were built in 1950. More than one hundred and fifty upscale antique shops are clustered on the ground level of two large apartment buildings. A pleasant walk from the Eiffel Tower, the area is clean, nicely planted, and well supplied with outdoor benches. There are many specialty shops, such as for clocks or nautical implements, and it's easier to get here than to Clignancourt. Also, Village Suisse is open on weekdays when Clignancourt is closed.

We looked longingly at some beautiful prayer rugs at the shop En 95. There are wonderful tapestries at Galerie Jabert—we've not seen them elsewhere, though perhaps we haven't looked hard enough. Galerie Meiji specializes in Japanese antiques, and FG MiniG has set up ranks of tiny toy soldiers in the shop window. Outside the courtyard but very close to the village, Aux Armes d'Autan has a large collection of pistols, swords, armor, and other warlike implements.

8TH ARRONDISSEMENT · CHAMPS-ÉLYSÉES

FOOD MARKETS

Batignolles Organic Open-Air Food Market · 105

Buying Organic · 108

Aguesseau Open-Air Food Market · 110

Treilhard Covered Food Market · 110
(formerly Marché Europe)

MARKETPLACES

Postage Stamp and Telephone Card Markets · 111

Antiques Courtyard · 114

Drouot Montaigne Auction House · 115

Place de la Madeleine Flower Market · 116

Batignolles Organic Open-Air Food Market

LE MARCHÉ BIOLOGIQUE DES BATIGNOLLES

*Boulevard des Batignolles from rue de Turin
to rue de Moscou, 8th and 17th arr.*

🚇 *Rome, Place de Clichy*

Saturday 8 am to 2 pm

This wonderful market has grown larger in recent years. It's the second largest of the city's three organic markets (see Buying Organic, p. 108). Many of the same merchants who sell at Batignolles on Saturday can be found at Raspail on Sunday. We think it's one of the better-kept secrets in Paris. Not many people who live outside the neighborhood are familiar with this market, which gives it extra charm, without the crowds, even on a sunny Saturday morning.

The Mayor's office classifies this market as in the 8th arrondissement, but in fact it straddles the eastern edge of the 17th. Prices are high, typically the case with organic products, but the market is a gem. Before Baron Haussmann transformed this area into a broad boulevard lined with majestic sandstone apartment buildings, it consisted of agricultural and hunting grounds. Aspects of that rural character still remain. In contrast to Raspail's

trendiness, the rhythms at Batignolles are more tranquil.

Once regarded as a small fringe market, le Marché Biologique des Batignolles is now firmly in the mainstream. Customers promenade along the tree-lined boulevard where vendors are lined up in two parallel rows. Every item is organic, from the vegetables and fruits to the cheeses and meats. The fish have not been bred in captivity, treated with artificial coloring, or frozen. We overhear animated conversations about production methods and seasonal specialties. Even the clothing that's sold here—shirts, dresses, sweaters, scarves—is made from organic cotton and mostly natural dyes.

Customers flock to buy seasonal, local items that are available only a couple of weeks each year, such as the first taste of white asparagus and early spring cheeses. We learned that even fresh-made butter tastes different in spring because cows that have been grazing on young grasses will produce milk with a brighter flavor. It made perfect sense after it was pointed out to us.

There's a high proportion of *producteurs* at this market—vendors who bring freshly picked produce straight from their farms. Dirt still clings to the carrots and potatoes. Several permit self-selection; others prefer to choose the produce for you. Provibio is one of several stands with excellent produce. Baskets of Spanish-grown avocados squeeze next to Île de France mounds of lettuce. We sample peppery tasting arugula (called *roquette*) and buy enough for several big salads.

There's also a good selection of wholesome breads, raw nuts, dried fruits, and local-production honeys and jams, as well as prepared foods made with healthy ingredients. Biopac sells sweet and savory vegetarian *tartes* made with whole-wheat crusts. We find it impossible to pass Les

Galatins without buying a sizzling hot potato-onion pancake. One of the most memorable stands belongs to Thérèse and Michel Beucher who sell organic apple and pear juices, sparkling cider, and Calvados, all hand-pressed at their farm in Normandy. Michel's skills extend beyond the orchard. He's a talented poet and singer who might, if he's in good spirits, break into a song that he composed. Indeed, he serenaded us for ten minutes.

Essential oils, soaps, teas, and cosmetics made from plants with healing properties abound at numerous stalls. Marie-Hélène Bégon sells sprouts and homeopathic remedies for allergies, insomnia, migraines, and other ailments. At another table, aromatic bath salts flecked with rose petals can be combined in custom blends. We left this market with a feeling of well-being, eager to dig into our sack bulging with healthy provisions.

BUYING ORGANIC
(TO BIO OR NOT TO BIO, THAT IS THE QUESTION)

The *bio* label—meaning organically grown or produced without synthetic chemicals—is popping up more than ever before. It's easy to find *bio* breads and grains, dairy, meats, fish, and wine in Paris's food markets. Even regular grocery stores are devoting additional shelf space to organic items of all kinds.

France has the dubious distinction of using more pesticides per capita than other European countries. Lately the press has been drawing the public's attention to the associated health risks and environmental dangers of all those chemicals. Early 2011 saw the first death of a French farmer that was officially linked to pesticide exposure. Others who are suffering from pesticide-related illnesses are coming forward.

Most open-air and covered markets have one or two stands that sell *agriculture biologique* (indicated by the AB label). But there are three weekly markets that are wholly dedicated to organic. The biggest is Raspail's Sunday market. Saturday's Batignolles market runs a close second, and the smaller one at Brancusi is another option. All the vegetables, fruits, meats and poultry, fish, and cheeses at those markets have been grown, fed, or produced according to organic guidelines. Compliance is strictly regulated. We were told that if a vendor is caught selling non-organic items under the *bio* label, punishment takes the form of stiff fines and possible jail time.

Items are especially well labeled at the city's organic markets, making it easy to identify the product's origin and place of production. (Ever since the breakout of Mad Cow disease, the French Ministry of Agriculture has enforced greater tracking and transparency of food sources.) There is also a higher proportion of *producteurs* at these markets who bring items directly from their own farms.

The French public is divided on the issue of how important it is to buy organic. Many are turned off by the substantially higher prices. On the other hand, customers who do buy organic feel it's worth the extra expense for the health of their family and the environment. Others prefer it because the animals are treated better. Some pay the premium because they believe they can taste a difference. Others contest the point. But judging by the strong turnout at the organic markets, the movement is healthy and growing.

Aguesseau Open-Air Food Market

LE MARCHÉ AGUESSEAU
Place de la Madeleine, 8th arr.
🚇 *Madeleine*
Tuesday and Friday 8 am to 1 pm

The heart of Paris is poorly served by open markets, so this one is a surprise. On the west side of the neo-classical Église de la Madeleine, this is the smallest of Parisian markets but worth a visit if one is curious or needs to shop.

Treilhard Covered Food Market

(formerly Marché Europe)

LE MARCHÉ COUVERT TREILHARD
1, rue Corvetto, 8th arr.
🚇 *Villiers, Europe*
Monday to Saturday 8:30 am to 8:30 pm; Sunday 8 am to 1 pm

This little market is situated on the ground floor of a modern building that occupies a small city block. Long windows with rounded corners and the imaginative use of glass block give it the aspect of a ship at sea. Inside are half a dozen stands in a spotless environment. The *charcutier* offers a different *plat du jour* each day that shoppers can take home and re-heat for dinner.

Postage Stamp and Telephone Card Markets

LE MARCHÉ DES TIMBRES (DE LA PHILATÉLIE)
Rue Gabriel from avenue Matignon to avenue de Marigny, 8th arr.
🚇 *Franklin Roosevelt, Champs Élysées-Clemenceau*
Thursday, Saturday, Sunday, and holidays 10 am to dusk

In a city of long-established markets, this is one of the oldest. Even if you're not a collector of postage stamps, an hour invested here will give you lessons in geography and history, and demonstrate art of high quality. Stamp dealers organize their material by country of origin and subject, and the logic of organization is itself an art. In addition to stamps sold singly or in sheets, franked or un-franked, you can find postcards with their original stamps, and envelopes with letters still inside them. There is a certain voyeuristic pleasure in reading the thoughts and cares of people long ago and far away. Each time we go back we are impressed by the diligence of these vendors, who sort and classify their stamps with magnifying glasses while they wait for serious collectors to approach them. We were struck by the exquisite rendering of tropical birds and flowers on the stamps of Mauritius and Madagascar.

CHEVAUX

Since they were introduced little more than a decade ago, phone cards carrying a small electronic puce or chip have swept across Europe. This market is still a rather informal institution compared with the adjacent stamp market, but it is growing at a brisk pace. Dealers work on park benches, on the hoods of cars, or on the curb where they display albums and boxes of cards for sale or trade. With an enormous variety of images and graphic designs, from sports figures to musicians and artists, from history to space travel and fantasy, phone cards quickly gained a place in the affections of collectors. They are avidly compared, traded, bought, and sold in a market that is becoming a fixture. Over the years, coins and postcards have crept into the fringes of this market, as well as a few postage stamps and, of all things, champagne caps.

Antiques Courtyard

LA COUR DES ANTIQUAIRES
54, rue Faubourg Saint-Honoré, 8th arr.
🚊 Champs-Élysées-Clemenceau
Tuesday to Sunday 10 am to 6 pm;
some shops close from noon to 2 pm or later

This collection of antique shops in a high-fashion street behind the Élysée Palace, the home of the French President, is worth more than a casual glance. The entrance is less inviting than one might expect, but eighteen sophisticated vendors offer a range of expensive furniture, art, and *objets décoratifs*.

Drouot Montaigne Auction House

L'HÔTEL DROUOT MONTAIGNE
15, avenue Montaigne, 8th arr.
🚊 *Alma-Marceau*
Viewing Monday to Friday 9:30 am to 1 pm;
sales 2 pm to 6 pm and other evening hours as announced

The location and architecture here are as different from Drouot Richelieu as fine china is from five-and-dime dishware. This branch of the auction house sells high-end French furnishings and decorative arts. The building resembles a small townhouse or a classy boutique hotel, in keeping with the neighbors in one of the most chic and expensive Parisian shopping streets. From the entrance hall of polished blond marble, a wide staircase with art nouveau banisters curves downward to a wood-paneled reception area. Stylish young women in smart red suits assist visitors who have legitimate business.

Place de la Madeleine Flower Market

LE MARCHÉ AUX FLEURS MADELEINE
East side of the Church of the Madeleine, 8th arr.
🚇 *Madeleine*
Open every day but Sunday from 8 am to 7:30 pm

This little flower market looks very much like the one at place des Ternes in the 17th arrondissement—the same weathered plywood siding and corrugated roof with the upper half of glass. There are very few plants, but a selection of cut flowers. The choice is adequate, if not overwhelming.

9TH ARRONDISSEMENT · OPÉRA

FOOD MARKETS

Galeries Lafayette Gourmet Food Hall · 119

Virtual Markets and Market Streets · 122

Anvers Open-Air Food Market · 125

Rue Cadet Market Street · 126

MARKETPLACES

Covered Passages · 127

Drouot Richelieu Auction House · 131

Citron praliné
シトロン・プラリネ

Macaron citron,
Crème chocolat blanc au citron,
Feuillantine pralinée

Galeries Lafayette Gourmet Food Hall

GALERIES LAFAYETTE GOURMET
Inside the Galeries Lafayette Men's Store on the 1st floor
48, boulevard Haussmann, 9th arr.
🚇 *Havre-Caumartin, Chaussée d'Antin-la Fayette*
Monday to Saturday 8:30 am to 9:30 pm

In the heart of the busy shopping district near Opéra Garnier stands one of Paris's finest merchandisers. Galeries Lafayette dates back to 1893 when two cousins opened a corner novelty store. Over the years it expanded to include several neighboring buildings on boulevard Haussmann and evolved into a grand department store with designer labels. Today it's recognized as a mecca for fashion shoppers, but it should not be overlooked by anyone interested in food. Galeries Lafayette's food hall is the Right Bank's answer to Bon Marché's La Grande Épicérie on the Left Bank. They are equally worthy as high temples to gourmet foods from France and elsewhere.

Expect to be tempted from the moment you set foot inside. Dalloyau's display of cakes and pastries sparkle like crown jewels. Their chessboard cake, a sweet-lover's nirvana, has checkerboard icing with dark and white chocolate pawns. For straight chocolate, you won't find much better than Jean-Paul Hévin's. And that's just for starters. If a sugar high hasn't stopped you cold in your tracks, continue a few steps and other high-quality brands will tempt, notably Eric Kayser breads and Japanese pastry maker Sadaharu Aoki, acclaimed for exotic flavored *macarons* and small tea cakes made with wasabi and green tea.

119

The general food hall spills open from there. Dairy cases and shelves are well-stocked with every imaginable item, as are counters for cheeses, meats, fresh fruits and vegetables, and prepared foods. It's a good spot to eat lunch, buy dinner, or stock up on food gifts. At least ten of the specialty food boutiques have adjoining seating areas. The low ceiling and department store music grated slightly on our nerves, but the sheer exhilaration of such bounty made the deeper impression. Next to the food hall is an extensive wine selection called La Bordeauxthèque, organized by region. Below it on the ground level is Layafette Organic, a new restaurant which sells all-organic items and is a pleasant respite with courtyard seating.

For a truly grand atmosphere in which to enjoy lunch or afternoon

tea, head a few doors down to Brasserie Printemps, on the top floor of Le Printemps department store at 64, boulevard Haussmann. The stunning circular atrium with its huge stained-glass cupola and intricately patterned iron balconies is an outstanding example of 1920s decorative arts. Le Printemps has its own version of gourmet foods. Small boutiques on the second floor of the home store are dedicated to upscale brands such as Ladurée, Hédiard, Mariage Frères, and La Maison du Chocolat. The food selection is not as extensive as what can be found at their competitor down the street; nevertheless, you're sure to come away neither empty-handed nor hungry.

Several neighborhoods have clusters of shops on the same or adjacent streets that feature similar kinds of goods. Knowing about such neighborhoods is useful if you're looking for a particular item; you can compare quality, cost, and condition without going all over the city.

Pets, plants, and garden tools can be found in the 1st arrondissement, quai de la Mégisserie, from rue Lavandières to rue des Bourdonnais (métro: Châtelet, Pont Neuf). Animal lovers come here to look and to dream. Vilmorin has the largest selection, and occupies most of a city block.

Shops selling low-priced women's clothing and goods by the yard begin in place du Caire, continue in passage du Caire, and end at boulevard Étienne-Marcel in the 2nd arrondissement (métro: Sentier, Bonne-Nouvelle, and Strasbourg-St-Denis). Also in the 2nd, shops dealing with coins, gold, and money (including exchange) are clustered on rue Vivienne, from boulevard Montmartre to rue Feydeau.

Sheet music and musical instruments can be found in the 8th arrondissement in rue de Rome and rue de Madrid, near the Gare Saint-Lazare (métro: St-Lazare). Leather and furs are sold on rue d'Hauteville in the 10th arrondissement (métro: Poissonnière). Also in the 10th, rue de Paradis contains a dozen shops selling stemware, glass, crystal, and china (métro: Gare de l'Est). Everything related to fabrics is available in shops on rue d'Orsel, near the Saint-Pierre fabric store (métro: Barbès-Rochechouart).

Rue du Faubourg Saint-Antoine, east of the Bastille opera house to the Saint-Antoine hospital in the 11th and 12th arrondissements, is a warren of low-end furniture stores (métro: Ledru-Rollin). The little passage du Chantier is especially intriguing. With its huge cobblestones it looks like a world that existed before the French Revolution.

Some streets, though not closed to vehicular traffic, are generally recognized as good places to go for bread and cheese, fruit and vegetables, meat and fish—essential provisions that keep a household going. Some have gained an almost clandestine reputation as "virtual" market streets. Rue de Buci intersects with rue de Seine in the 6th. An attractive array of shops and cafés clusters around this corner. The street is often so full of pedestrians that it might as well be classified as such (métro: Mabillon).

One of the best informal market streets is rue des Martyrs, from rue de la Vieuville in the 18th arrondissement to rue Saint-Lazare/rue Lamartine in the 9th, especially around boulevard de Clichy/boulevard Rochechouart. Rue Lepic, also in the 18th arrondissement east of the Montmartre cemetery, is similarly blessed. It makes its crooked way from rue Léandre to rue Ravignan (métro: Abbesses, Lamarck Caulaincourt).

In the 14th arrondissement, rue Delambre is not much to look at, but it has an outstanding cheese shop and butcher, and one of the best places in the city to buy a fresh baguette. The street begins at the Edgar Quinet métro entrance, and ends at the boulevard du Montparnasse.

The French word for a low-price outlet is *stock*. The word is found on shop-fronts in the 14th arrondissement, on rue d'Alésia from place Victor et Hélène Basch to rue Didot (métro: Alésia). Clothing has been *dégriffé*, meaning that the original label has been removed and the goods offered at reduced prices.

Anvers Open-Air Food Market

LE MARCHÉ ANVERS

Place d'Anvers, between boulevard de Rochechouart and
avenue Trudaine, 9th arr.

🚊 *Anvers*

Friday 3 pm to 8:30 pm

Marché Anvers is an example of an afternoon food market at its best. Residents of the 9th and the 18th arrondissements pause on their way home from work or while their children play in the adjacent park. Numerous producers sell homemade specialties. The beret-clad Monsieur Roger of La Ferme de la Prairie offers tastes of goat cheese. For sausages, Auvergne is a good bet. Shoppers line up at Warin for other meats.

Vegetables, fruits, fish, cheese, rotisserie chickens, and flowers abound with several vendors to choose from in each category. This market has good quality products and plenty of them. Step away from the stalls and the leafy canopy of chestnut trees to admire the majestic grey-white domes of la Basilique du Sacré Coeur hovering over the rooftops.

Rue Cadet Market Street

LA RUE CADET

From rue du Faubourg Montmartre to rue la Fayette, 9th arr.

🚋 *Cadet*

Tuesday to Saturday 10 am to 6 pm; Sunday morning

This narrow street at first seems dark and forbidding, but on closer examination it becomes a friendly shopping street. Several bookstores cater to a variety of interests. A bagel shop, butcher, *charcuterie*, *fromagerie*, produce stand, shoe repair shop, hardware store, and sidewalk cafés round out the offerings. A hodgepodge of architectural styles come together here, from the modern curved aluminum and glass structure of the Freemasons Museum to the eighteenth-century stone building across the street. The handsome original shop of a small *confiserie-épicerie*, À La Mère de Famille, stands out at the intersection with rue du Faubourg Montmartre. It opened here in 1761 and now has several other locations.

Covered Passages

Passage Jouffroy-Verdeau, completed in 1846, begins on the north side of boulevard Montmartre and goes straight through to rue de Provence. Spend a few minutes in Le Grenier aux Livres, where you can turn the pages of fine old books, skim some new ones as well, and find colorful and amusing calendars. You may stop for a bite of lunch at the pleasant

Restaurant Verdeau, the tiny, authentic Bistro Verdeau, or the restaurant l'Arbre à Cannelle.

Peek into the Hôtel Chopin, no bigger than a mouse, with its fine nineteenth-century façade. Next door is the Musée Grévin, a wax museum of historical and contemporary figures to rival Madame Tussaud's in London, plus distorting mirrors and a magic show for kids of all ages. Pain d'Epice has children's toys and fanciful stuffed figures. The adjacent Comptoir de la Famille sells bowls, baskets, hand towels, and oil and vinegar cruets.

(See also 2nd arrondissement, p. 45, for a historical note on Covered Passages.)

Drouot Richelieu Auction House

L'HÔTEL DROUOT RICHELIEU

9, rue Drouot, 9th arr.

🚇 *Richelieu Drouot*

Viewing: Monday to Friday 11 am to 6 pm;

Auctions: Monday to Friday 1 pm to 6 pm

The Drouot Auction House stands at the corner of rue Drouot and rue Rossini, its location since 1852. While the neighborhood has become a bit seamy, the auction house lives on like an elderly gentleman in a deteriorating neighborhood.

The building itself seems an architectural anomaly with a vaguely modern artistic pedigree. The sales rooms were renovated in 1980.

Above and below the ground level, the floors are covered with squares of red carpet, suggesting they may need to be replaced often. The walls in the viewing rooms are covered with heavy red material, to easily and quickly change exhibits.

Some exhibition rooms are sublet to specialists in various markets. We observed that the objects for auction at the basement level were barely a cut above flea-market goods, while on the ground floor and first floor there was a

definite improvement in quality. Drouot-related offices for giving estimates or handling special materials dominate much of the surrounding neighborhood.

Traditionally, women employees at Hôtel Drouot wore black skirts and red scarves, and men wore black suits with red collars—but it's all red tee-shirts now. In 1860, when Sardinia ceded Savoy to France, the Savoyards acquired the exclusive right to transport art objects and to handle them at auction. Since then, entry to the profession has been possible only when a vacancy occurs through retirement or resignation.

Auctions are open to the public, and auction information is published in *PariScope*, available at news kiosks (a new issue comes out every Wednesday). The French Assembly passed a law in 2001 that repealed the restriction of auction purchases to French nationals. Subsequently, both Sotheby's and Christie's opened sales rooms in Paris. Drouot responded to this challenge by opening an additional sales site in the northern part of the city (64, rue Doudeauville, 18th arrondissement) and a facility for auto sales called Drouot-Véhicules.

10TH ARRONDISSEMENT · GARE DU NORD

FOOD MARKETS

Saint-Quentin Covered Food Market · 137

Victor Baltard, Architect · 139

Alibert Open-Air Food Market · 141

Saint-Martin Covered Food Market · 142

Saint-Quentin Covered Food Market

LE MARCHÉ COUVERT SAINT-QUENTIN

85 bis, boulevard Magenta (at corner of rue de Chabrol), 10th arr.

🚇 *Gare de l'Est*

Tuesday to Saturday 9 am to 1 pm, 4 pm to 7:30 pm;

Sunday 8:30 am to 1:30 pm

Some of the covered markets feel cramped and dreary, but Saint-Quentin stands out for its stunning architecture. Located in a busy neighborhood near Gare de l'Est and Gare du Nord, this is the largest of the covered markets. Its nineteenth-century façade combines brick, wood, glass, steel, and ironwork and makes a handsome appearance from the street. Designed by the architect Rabourdin, the structure attracts architecture buffs since it's an outstanding example of the Baltard style (see p. 139), and one of the few covered markets in this style that still exists.

Step inside and let your gaze be drawn upward. Unfortunately the maze of stands doesn't permit clear sight lines, but you'll catch glimpses of the soaring ceiling. Iron roof-trusses are set on cast-iron capitals with a Corinthian motif. Outside light pours in through glass walls that are set into grand steel arches. Even if you have no market items to purchase, it's worth a detour to see this architectural gem. But if you do have a shopping list, all the better. One can find the usual market foods and beverages, as well as a shoe repair and key shop, a hardware store, and Portuguese, Italian, and Lebanese take-out dishes. Friendly vendors have developed a loyal clientele.

At the rue Cabrol entrance, Boucherie Jouve sells excellent quality meat. Monsieur Jouve looked comfortable in the bloodied apron slung over one shoulder. He concentrated on sharpening knives as he peered out from under a brown plaid beret and leaned over his thick *billot* (butcher's block), its surface worn smooth from over forty years of operating this stand. The lean and tender beef that he and his wife sell comes from the Blonde d'Aquitaine cattle in southwestern France.

At Rôtisserie Volaille, we happened to catch the meticulous Monsieur Devineau marinating rabbit in Maille mustard and *crème fraîche* d'Isigny before grilling it. Fromagerie Quiécout sells not only cheeses but also a selection of jams, jellies, juices, and wines. A few steps away at *traiteur* Daniel Verin, varieties of salami, pâté, and *rillettes* of goose, duck, and pork are displayed along with prepared dishes such as *choucroute* cooked with Riesling and juniper berries, and pickled salads.

On the opposite side of the market is Terres de Bières, a boutique of artisanal beers from France and Belgium, including organic beers. Monsieur Giannoni observes that people are buying more beer for consumption at home (as opposed to cafés, where they're relatively expensive). French microbreweries are on the rise. The warm, earthy tones and design of his shop create the semblance of a beer cave, or cellar, and shrink the looming scale of the market building down to a cozy, hospitable size.

VICTOR BALTARD, ARCHITECT (1805-1874)

The face of Paris in the nineteenth century was changed by several men, of whom the best known is Eugène Haussmann, the planner of the *grands boulevards*, parks, and squares that define the modern city. Another was one of Haussmann's closest friends and associates, Victor Baltard, who had much to do with the way Paris looked and worked then and persists today.

The son of Louis-Pierre Baltard, a renowned architect, artist, and member of the faculty of the École des Beaux Arts, Victor distinguished himself early in life by submitting the winning design for the tomb of Napoléon I. He was denied the commission because, at 36, he was considered too young and inexperienced. He entered the government architectural service and rose rapidly, partly as a result of his friendship with Haussmann, to become chief architect of the city of Paris. In this capacity he designed the city hall that was destroyed by fire in 1871.

Baltard's best-known work was Les Halles (the central food market that was moved to Rungis). The initial design had poor traffic patterns and bad ventilation. After a personal visit by Napoléon III, construction was halted. Working with his colleague Félix-Emmanuel Callet, Baltard improved the design, and the first of ten buildings was completed in 1853. His great innovation was a glass and iron umbrella-shaped roof that maximized natural light and ventilation. This style was later used in the construction of covered neighborhood markets, of which Saint-Quentin, Saint-Martin, and La Chapelle still exist.

In addition to les Halles, Baltard designed the church of Saint-Augustin, on the boulevard Malesherbes. It was the first time that an iron frame was used inside a French church as a decorative as well as a structural feature. By the end of a long and celebrated career he had become, like his father, professor of architectural theory at the École des Beaux Arts. Published widely and acclaimed for his work, Baltard became an Officer of the Legion of Honor and was elected to the Institut de France.

Alibert Open-Air Food Market

LE MARCHÉ ALIBERT

Rue Alibert, odd-numbered side, between rue Claude Vellefaux and rue Bichat, 10th arr.

🚇 *Goncourt*

Sunday 8 am to 1 pm

A tiny market along a narrow sidewalk with scarcely room to maneuver, this would be worth a visit only for those staying in the neighborhood. Two vegetable vendors, a butcher, and a flower stall make up the regular stands, plus a mattress-seller who also re-canes chairs.

Saint-Martin Covered Food Market

LE MARCHÉ COUVERT SAINT-MARTIN

31-33, rue du Château d'Eau, 10th arr.

🚇 *Château d'Eau*

Tuesday to Friday 9:30 am to 1 pm, 4 pm to 7:30 pm;

Saturday 9 am to 7:30 pm; Sunday 9 am to 1:30 pm

This covered market lies in the midst of a diverse neighborhood with warrens of passageways and ethnic restaurants. Large stone portals of the old market have been re-erected in front of a modern building as a symbol of the vanished past. Inside, stands offer flowers, meat, cheese, fruit, vegetables (including one selling organic produce), and a particular-

ly well-stocked fish market with a good selection of oysters. German specialties, otherwise hard to find in Paris, fill the shelves at Tante Emma-Laden in the rear. The gregarious owner, Philippe Même, has been dubbed "the Mozart of grilled sausages" because they are so good. You can sample them at picnic tables adjoining his shop.

11TH ARRONDISSEMENT ✦ BASTILLE

FOOD MARKETS

Bastille Open-Air Food Market ✦ 145
(also known as Richard Lenoir)

Belleville Open-Air Food Market ✦ 148

Charonne Open-Air Food Market ✦ 150

Popincourt Open-Air Food Market ✦ 151

MARKETPLACES

Bastille Arts and Crafts Market ✦ 152

Bastille Open-Air Food Market
(also known as Richard Lenoir)

LE MARCHÉ BASTILLE

Boulevard Richard Lenoir from rue Amelot to rue Saint-Sabin, 11th arr.

🚇 *Bastille*

Thursday 8 am to 1:30 pm; Sunday 8 am to 2 pm

A stone's throw from where the Bastille prison was stormed by the proletariat in 1789, thus igniting the French Revolution, one now finds a vibrant marketplace. It reflects in some ways the history of this site, attracting a dynamic mix of French society—rich and poor, working and unemployed. The prison was destroyed, but a large column at place de la Bastille commemorates the uprising that took place here and changed history forever.

On market days, stalls stretch for blocks down the middle of tree-lined boulevard Richard Lenoir. In fact, this market used to be called Richard Lenoir, and many still refer to it that way. Roughly 200 sellers attend, making it one of Paris's largest and liveliest. A carnival atmosphere sets the tone at the starting point, where a carousel and games catch children's attention; nearby stands selling clothing, soaps, jewelry, and African sculpture attract

145

adults. Three aisles of vendors extend for blocks. Noisy chatter greets shoppers at the southern end. One merchant calls out "*un eurrro*," trilling the "r" and sounding like a Citroën's starter straining to turn over.

Produce vendors bring unusual seasonal items, such as the thistle-like cardoon which is a relative of the artichoke. Every fresh herb imaginable is sold here—dried bunches remind us of shaving brushes. In the fall there is a profusion of game, and the wild mushrooms are utterly compelling: *cèpes* as big as our hands, like those we've hunted on the mountain slopes of Provence. Abundant displays of vegetables and fruits range from a conventional mix to more local specialties.

Poissonnerie Lorenzo, recognizable by the stars on its canopy, specializes in large pieces of fish, notably sea bass, sole, and sea bream. Monsieur Lorenzo and his sons go to Rungis in the wee hours of the morning to pick the best selection. "Qualité Extra Petits Bateaux" on the labels indicate that the fish were caught on hand-lines by small French fishing boats. At Poissonerie Maria, we saw a customer use a pole to poke at the exact filets she wanted for dinner that night. Workers in blue aprons stood at a table skinning and gutting. A saleswoman yelled "*dos de cabillaud*!" urging them to hasten their slicing of codfish so she could refill the display.

Excellent cheese makers also regularly attend this market. Ferme de la Brie sells their farm-made *brie de Meaux*, *fromage blanc*, *crème fraîche*, and *pur chèvre au lait cru* (raw milk goat cheese), along with other outstanding cheeses. Michel Lucien took his knife to a chunk of *tomme de chèvre* and passed around samples. His daughter pinched rounds of goat cheese to select the appropriate ripeness to satisfy a customer who wanted to serve it in two days.

Part of the fun is stumbling upon specialty producers, such as Bar à Harengs that sells thirty varieties of sweet or spicy marinated herrings. Customers also wait their turn at Taranga for curries and other traditional African dishes. Portuguese and Italian specialties can be found, as well as small-batch wines from Bordeaux and the Loire valley.

Shoes, clothing, CDs, and cooking gadgets are set out in colorful displays. Throngs of customers take advantage of the deals, giving a modern interpretation to the storming of the Bastille.

Along the walkway, clusters of benches and fountains provide incentive to pause for a rest. They attract musicians too. A beret-clad organ grinder sang traditional French ballads and hammed it up with the crowd while feeding perforated music cards through his *orgue de barbarie* (street organ). Nearby a man tootled on his piccolo while dancing unsteadily. We couldn't tell if he was intoxicated by the music or by a bottle no longer in view. Regardless, a gaiety infuses this market and people are drawn to it as much for fun as for food.

We retreated to one of the cafés that serve as popular meeting points and watering holes around place de la Bastille with its wide perspective. Fortified with an espresso and crispy *palmier* cookie, we imagined how different the scene looked during the events that occurred here over two centuries ago.

Belleville Open-Air Food Market

LE MARCHÉ BELLEVILLE

Boulevard de Belleville, rue du Faubourg du Temple/rue de Belleville to rue Oberkampf/rue de Ménilmontant, 11th arr.

🚊 *Belleville, Couronnes, Ménilmontant*

Tuesday and Friday 8 am to 1:30 pm

Four arrondissements—the 10th, 11th, 19th, and 20th—come together at the northern end of this market, creating a hectic hub where different cultures mingle. Clusters of men hawk their goods to Asian couples pushing carts, tall North African women in brightly colored headdresses, and Muslim women in dark burkas. This is one of the markets where commerce tends to divide along gender lines: men generally sell, women generally buy.

Belleville is an exciting place to experience an outdoor market at full tilt and to buy inexpensive items in bulk. But don't expect to find a comfortable spot on the sidelines or to engage with vendors in small talk. Instead you'll be swept into a surging stream of shoppers, elbows jostling as you pass. There are occasional calm eddies before the next current pushes you onward. It doesn't feel unsafe, but rather there's the exhilaration of a noisy, energetic marketplace. People come here to shop, not to socialize.

Stalls sell mostly fruits and vegetables along several city blocks that stretch across three métro stations, but there's also fish, Halal meats, and cheese. At intersections, men sell bunches of parsley, mint, cilantro, and other fresh herbs from wooden bins. Prices decline as the hours pass and vendors rush to deplete their inventories. Near closing time, we watched one grab his blackboards, squeeze orange juice on them, rub his shirt cuff over the lettering to erase the numbers, and write new prices at half the amount. There are plenty of cheap household goods, candy, and clothing—anything from lacy undergarments to full-length embroidered dresses.

Part of the fun is listening to the sellers. Repeated cries of "*un euro! un!*" blend to create spellbinding incantations. Ripe oranges, avocados, and pumpkins are slashed through the navel and split open to expose their fleshy innards. Whether they're tasted or simply offered as evidence of quality, it's one more way to entice customers from the passing stream.

Charonne Open-Air Food Market

LE MARCHÉ CHARONNE

*Boulevard de Charonne between rue de Charonne and
rue Alexandre Dumas, 11th arr.*

🚇 *Alexandre Dumas*

Wednesday 8 am to 1:30 pm; Saturday 8 am to 2 pm

A smaller and calmer market, Marché Charonne has more of a village feel to it than the boisterous ambience at nearby Aligre or Belleville markets. You can buy fish fresh from Normandy at Chez Laurent. Michel Chamillard has *choucroute*, duckling stuffed with prunes, and a sizzling rotisserie with a variety of poultry, rabbit, and turkey legs on his spits. Tiny white potatoes are heaped in the hot fat underneath. The hawking of fresh fruit goes like this: "*Fraises, Mesdames, très, très belles et très solides!*" Grandjean's staff, dressed in red shirts and white aprons, offer ready-to-eat dishes, including the ever-popular *brandade de morue*, sauté of pork with Indian spices, veal tongue with mushrooms, and beef with carrots.

Popincourt Open-Air Food Market

LE MARCHÉ POPINCOURT

*Boulevard Richard Lenoir from rue Jean-Pierre Timbaud to
rue Oberkampf, 11th arr.*

🚇 *Oberkampf*

Tuesday and Friday 8 am to 1:30 pm

This spacious market is lined with large leafy trees and graced by plantings and fountains that run down the center.

A man selling fruits and unfiltered juices from his orchard north of Paris travels about thirty miles to bring them to regular customers at this market. Certain times of year he has sparkling rhubarb cider in addition to traditional apple varieties. Other specialties that can be found at this friendly market include freshly roasted coffee beans, and pickled fish, with an especially tasty pickled herring.

The vendor of a staggering display of buttons, patches, threads, toggles, tools, and curiosities related to sewing reviewed for us the decline of his business due to changes in style and the availability of ready-made clothing. Fishmongers do well here; four of them each had long queues of clients. One stand offered a large selection of dried fruit, including sugar-cured kumquats.

Bastille Arts and Crafts Market

LE MARCHÉ DE LA CRÉATION BASTILLE
Median plaza, Boulevard Richard Lenoir, 11th arr.
🚇 *Bastille, Breguet-Sabin*
Saturday 9 am to 6 pm

A small arts and crafts market is set up on the median plaza where the Bastille open-air food market is located. It is smaller in scale than the arts and crafts market in the 14th arrondissement on Sundays, but it makes a pleasurable outing on a Saturday morning, and one can meet a different set of Parisian artists and see a range of styles (as well as a range in quality).

12TH ARRONDISSEMENT • BERCY

FOOD MARKETS

Beauvau Covered Food Market • 155

Rue d'Aligre Market Street • 159

Bercy Open-Air Food Market • 162

Cours de Vincennes Open-Air Food Market • 163

Daumesnil Open-Air Food Market • 164

Ledru-Rollin Open-Air Food Market • 164

Poniatowski Open-Air Food Market • 165

Saint-Eloi Open-Air Food Market • 165

MARKETPLACES

Viaduct Arts and Crafts Shops • 167

Beauvau Covered Food Market

LE MARCHÉ COUVERT BEAUVAU
Place d'Aligre, 12th arr.

🚇 *Ledru-Rollin*

Tuesday to Saturday 9 am to 1 pm, 4 pm to 7:30 pm;
Sunday 8:30 am to 1:30 pm

The covered food market Beauvau stands at the heart of place d'Aligre. After walking through the frenzied street market pulsating right outside its doors, a step inside the building transports you to a different world. It's quieter, but with a steady and strong flow of commerce.

A registered historic site, the Beauvau market has changed little in two hundred years. It is the second-oldest covered market (after Enfants Rouges) and one of the most striking. Huge limestone columns support a massive roof. Crisscrossing wooden roof beams offset the weight of the exterior by bringing light and airiness to the lofty overhead space. Some say the market was originally a stable and the fountain at its center was a drinking trough. Whether or not that's historically accurate, what's undisputed is that the fountain is no mere decoration but a practical, cast iron monolith that supplies merchants and cleaning crews with washing water. Signs of wear in the stones underfoot verify that generations of Parisians have

shopped here for their market goods.

Quality vendors occupy individual stalls each with its own kitchen and storage space. We found Sur les Quais an enchanting shop and a good source for gifts. Owner Paul Vautrin left his job as an engineer to focus on his higher passion: gastronomy. He developed the concept of sprayable oils and also of packaging unusual flavors of mustard in aluminum tubes so they stay fresh longer. His newest idea is spices in small quantities, sold in collectible glass jars at reasonable prices, with simple explanations and recipes attached.

Angelillo, located by the fountain and recognizable by the deer head mounted on the wall, sells every kind of dressed poultry, including fresh *magret* (duck breast) and turkey parts. The excellent butcher Michel Brunon has *charcuterie* and animal parts hanging from large hooks above his stall. He is one of the best for *cheval* (horse meat), which is making a comeback among foodies.

Hardouin/Langlet displays 300 varieties of cheese during the weekdays and 400 on the weekend, recalling President de Gaulle's memorable observation. They also have sliced Poilâne bread, *feuilletes* (flaky pastry) *au Roquefort*, and wines that pair nicely with their cheeses for those in search of instant picnic fare.

Rounding out the offerings are several fresh produce stands with slightly higher prices (and corresponding quality) compared to those outside, fishmongers, Italian specialties, and a beer seller who specializes in microbrews. Before leaving this pleasant oasis, brace yourself for the commotion of Marché d'Aligre that awaits as soon as you pass through the doors.

Rue d'Aligre Market Street

LE MARCHÉ RUE D'ALIGRE
Rue d'Aligre from rue Crozatier to rue de Charenton, 12th arr.
🚇 *Ledru-Rollin*
Tuesday to Sunday 8 am to 1:30 pm

This heads the list for many Parisians, as one of the city's best market streets and certainly one of the oldest. Ask people their weekend plans and often a favorite activity is shopping at Aligre followed by a meal with friends at one of the nearby restaurants. Every day but Monday, a fantastic medley of people, products, and food magically appears, then disappears by early afternoon.

The area actually combines three different markets: the street market that runs almost the entire length of rue d'Aligre; the Beauvau covered market in place d'Aligre (see p. 155); and a flea market that spreads out in a semicircle behind the clock tower. No fancy outfits here, but racks and piles of simple cotton clothing along with inexpensive nicknacks. One can see a great deal of inexpensive *brocante* in half an hour's stroll.

Take a gander at the whole market before making purchases, since there's much to choose from and prices vary. The main concentration of fruit and vegetable stands runs between rue Crozatier and place d'Aligre. Behind them a variety of delicatessens, fishmongers, and conventional stores double the density of shopping opportunities. Weave in and out between the permanent shops and the temporary stalls, dodging the crates that line the curbs. Numerous Halal butchers, more produce stands, and a traditional French butcher beckon at the other end of the street. A flower stand near the entrance to the covered market seems to have an unlimited selection at popular prices. La Graineterie du Marché at 8, place d'Aligre is one of the oldest shops in the area and has a friendly English-speaking owner, Jose. It is a good source for organic grains, garden seeds, or market bags that you'll want to keep.

Shoppers of all types, ages, and ethnicities converge here. Mothers and nannies push infants in strollers. Children wobble by on bicycles and brake quickly for pieces of sliced fruit that are generously handed out. Clusters of men, each wearing a classic *fez*, congregate to discuss the day's news. Everyone seems to find satisfaction in the Marché d'Aligre, which is doubtless the reason for its reputation.

Young men hawk their piles of vegetables and fruits, shouting out "*un euro!*" and "*allez!*" offering samples of the ripest. Their strategy succeeds: We bought peaches, watermelon, and cherries after tasting their sweetness, even though our bag was already heavy with other purchases. Hard bargaining goes along with rock-bottom prices if you buy in quantity. But you've got to be on your toes. Commerce is quick, and the vendors won't coddle you. Keep a watchful eye when buying produce so that no clunkers from the backs of the piles get slipped into the bag. If merchants sometimes seem a bit impatient, it may be due to the high proportion of onlookers relative to shoppers. When you stop to take a picture, don't be surprised if this fast-moving crowd bumps you around.

As closing time approaches, merchants start taking down their stands while lowering the price of remaining produce, happier to sell it cheap than to cart it home. Boxes of berries and fruit in season come down in price until finally a whole crateful goes for a steal. If you don't

mind the frenzy, it can be worth the wait.

Then comes the well-orchestrated cleanup. Foot soldiers clad in green move down the sidewalks and deploy their plastic brooms. Streams of water cascade through the street, scattering the last of the shoppers. A few women and children pick through the remains. Soon the trash is swept into heaps, shoveled into trucks, and only the damp street steaming quietly in the sun shows that there was a market here at all.

Bercy Open-Air Food Market

LE MARCHÉ BERCY

Place Lachambeaudie and rue du Baron Le Roy, 12th arr.

🚇 *Dugommier*

Wednesday 3 pm to 8 pm; Sunday 8 am to 2 pm

Opened in February 2001, this market serves a part of Paris that is beginning to develop as a residential area relatively close to the city center. It's small, but there is at least one of every kind of vendor. Bercy once lay outside the city and was used by shippers who stored wine here to avoid city taxes. This market celebrates the products of the department of Aveyron, in the south of France, known for its Saturday markets and a local wine that marries well with the famous cheese of the region, Roquefort.

Cours de Vincennes Open-Air Food Market

LE MARCHÉ COURS DE VINCENNES
*Cours de Vincennes from boulevard de Picpus to
avenue Dr. Arnold Netter, 12th and 20th arr.*
🚇 *Nation, Porte de Vincennes*
Wednesday 8 am to 1:30 pm; Saturday 8 am to 2 pm

This enormous market stretches for several blocks alongside the cours de Vincennes, a busy thoroughfare that connects the 12th and 20th arrondissements. Large apartment complexes line the street, some contemporary with straight walls and square corners, others more modern with curved balconies. Traffic noise is at first offensive, but upon entering the market with stalls on each side, vendors' voices overpower all else as they call out to passersby. Prices span a range, but it's possible to find affordable, good-quality produce and clothing. The offal vendor packs four kinds of tongue, as well as sheep and veal brains in plastic containers. One baker sells a pound cake called Quatre-Quarts, which contains a kilo each of flour, butter, sugar, and eggs.

Daumesnil Open-Air Food Market

LE MARCHÉ DAUMESNIL
Boulevard de Reuilly between place Félix Eboué and
rue de Charenton, 12th arr.
🚇 *Daumesnil, Dugommier*
Tuesday and Friday 8 am to 1:30 pm

This immense and busy market serves a neighborhood of apartment buildings. A double row of sycamores on both sides of the street shades the entire market. Most shoppers are older men and women, who share friendly greetings and good-natured gossip.

Ledru-Rollin Open-Air Food Market

LE MARCHÉ LEDRU-ROLLIN
Even-numbered side of avenue Ledru-Rollin,
between rue de Lyon and rue de Bercy, 12th arr.
🚇 *Gare de Lyon, Quai de la Rapée*
Thursday 8 am to 1:30 pm; Saturday 8 am to 2 pm

A sycamore-lined thoroughfare just a few blocks from Gare de Lyon is home to an unpretentious market. Half a dozen restaurants in the area prosper from the provisions available to them—Le Frégate for seafood, Le Quincy for specialties of the Auvergne, À la Biche au Bois for reliable game dishes. The Viaduc des Arts (see p. 167) is only a block away.

Poniatowski Open-Air Food Market

LE MARCHÉ PONIATOWSKI
Odd-numbered side of boulevard Poniatowski
from avenue Daumesnil to rue Picpus, 12th arr.
🚇 *Porte Dorée*
Thursday 8 am to 1 pm; Sunday 8 am to 2 pm

This neighborhood market is rather remote, but no doubt provides comfort and convenience for local residents. There are not many stands here, or much to distinguish them from similar vendors elsewhere. A McDonald's on the corner is a bit disconcerting.

Saint-Eloi Open-Air Food Market

LE MARCHÉ SAINT-ELOI
36-38, rue de Reuilly,
in the triangle created by rue du Col and rue Rozanoff, 12th arr.
🚇 *Reuilly-Diderot, Montgallet*
Thursday 8 am to 1:30 pm; Sunday 8 am to 2 pm

The arcade covering this market is worth something in bad weather. Vegetable, fish, and meat vendors look a bit fatigued, perhaps from the effort of competition with the Casino Supermarket across the street.

Viaduct Arts and Crafts Shops

LE VIADUC DES ARTS

Avenue Daumesnil, from avenue Ledru-Rollin to rue Montgallet, 12th arr.

🚇 *Bastille, Gare de Lyon*

Tuesday to Saturday 10 am to 6 pm;

however, some shops open later, stay open longer, and have Sunday hours

A smart and aesthetically pleasing restoration of an abandoned railroad viaduct was completed in 1998 as a joint effort of the city of Paris and the government of the 12th arrondissement. Fifty-six arched spaces house a variety of shops and services devoted to decorative arts and home design.

The Viaduct has brought many benefits to residents and businesses in the neighborhood, though expectations such as low-rent housing have been sacrificed. Nevertheless, the restoration has given a needed facelift and an economic boost to a tired part of Paris. The general orientation of these elegant shops is home furnishings, restoration, and fashion, which still leaves considerable room for personal shopping. For example, some spaces have become studios where original furniture, lace, and gold-embossed leather-bound books are created. Le Bonheur des Dames has an assortment of books, boxes, and stuffed bunnies, plus bangles and beads to dress up a garment or a piece of furniture. Mahia Kent weaves scarves, jackets, and coats on a large and impressive hand-loom.

Cécile et Jeanne have created some of the most striking affordable jewelry we have seen in Paris, as well as smart handbags. Michel Pintado has original sculptures and paintings. Take a look at the fabric flowers for fashion and decoration by Guillet (in Paris since 1896). Are you in the market for a guitar or a bass viol? If so, Atelier Dupont is the place to go. You can rent a party costume at Le Vestiaire, or find your heart's delight for the kitchen at l'Univers de la Cuisine. The most original item we saw was at Zephyr. Holographic images are captured in blocks of optical glass. These artisans can represent a photo of a child or loved one in a way that is extraordinarily realistic and even a bit spooky.

For coffee, tea, or a bite of lunch, stop at the Café l'Arrosoir at boulevard Diderot, or Le Viaduc Café at rue Abel. Both offer reliable bistro dishes, and outdoor seating in good weather.

A striking feature of the Viaduct is the pedestrian walkway atop the old right-of-way. It begins behind the new opera house at place de la Bastille, and ends in the Jardin de Reuilly about a mile away. Both sides of the path are thickly planted with bamboo, pyracantha, roses, and viburnum. There are bridges, benches, fountains, convenient stairways to the street, and an elevator for the handicapped. Small niches facing south are enticing on a sunny day. Young locust trees have fulfilled their promise and grown large and leafy; climbing roses are reaching for the tops of their trellises. This is among the most attractive public gardens in Paris, one of the loveliest and most soothing in this busy city. It's open from 8 am until 9 pm.

13TH ARRONDISSEMENT · NATIONAL LIBRARY

FOOD MARKETS

Alésia Open-Air Food Market · 1 7 0

Auguste-Blanqui Open-Air Food Market · 1 7 1

Bobillot Open-Air Food Market · 1 7 4

Jeanne d'Arc Open-Air Food Market · 1 7 4

Maison-Blanche Open-Air Food Market · 1 7 5

Paris Rive Gauche Open-Air Food Market · 1 7 5

Salpêtrière Open-Air Food Market · 1 7 6

Vincent Auriol Open-Air Food Market · 1 7 6

Alésia Open-Air Food Market

LE MARCHÉ ALÉSIA

From place Coluche, even-numbered side of rue de la Glacière,
continues on rue de la Santé from number 137 to the end, 13th arr.

🚇 *Glacière, Corvisart*

Wednesday and Saturday 8 am to 1 pm

Tall, lacy acacia trees maintain a comfortable temperature and create pleasant ambient light. The market offers the usual fare and is easy to stroll and absorb, as it spreads out against a fence along the sidewalk of rue de la Glacière. The cheese stand has wheels of Comté and Emmenthal big enough to feed *tout le quartier*.

Auguste-Blanqui Open-Air Food Market

LE MARCHÉ AUGUSTE-BLANQUI

Boulevard Auguste-Blanqui from place d'Italie to rue Barrault, 13th arr.

🚇 *Place d'Italie*

Tuesday and Friday 8 am to 1:30 pm; Sunday 8 am to 2 pm

During the workweek, place d'Italie throbs with traffic around its rotary. People stream in and out of the large commercial complex that anchors one corner, and the Tuesday food market is relatively tranquil. On Sundays, the dynamic reverses with the pulse of activity located in the market as it fills with locals who come to do their shopping. This large market has a very pleasant atmosphere and winds along a gentle slope for several tree-lined blocks. Merchants who scoop out helpings of Lebanese, Italian, Portuguese, Thai, and Chinese dishes reflect the multi-ethnic backgrounds of the shoppers.

Boucherie Olivier sells excellent meats. C'Bio has all organic items. An artisanal baker across the aisle sells breads and fruit *clafoutis*. We picked up a Quatre-Quarts pound cake sweetened with fresh apricots, but had a hard time choosing between it and the brownie-like chocolate

version. Several local producers bring their own garden harvest—heirloom tomatoes at Les Serres de la Tretoire and superb vegetables at Earl Raehm, to name a couple. We bought a pair of comfortable shoes at a good price from a vendor who permits customers to try them on, and then were reinvigorated enough to continue strolling along a seemingly endless row of stands.

Bobillot Open-Air Food Market

LE MARCHÉ BOBILLOT
On the sidewalk of rue Bobillot between place de Rungis and rue de la Colonie, 13th arr.
🚇 *Tolbiac, Maison Blanche*
Tuesday and Friday 8 am to 1 pm

Old sycamore trees shade this relaxed and friendly market. There is a pretty park near the place de Rungis. High school students come and go through a gate in the middle of the market, enlivening the site.

Jeanne d'Arc Open-Air Food Market

LE MARCHÉ JEANNE D´ARC
Both sides of the church Notre Dame de la Gare, place Jeanne d'Arc, 13th arr.
🚇 *Nationale, Chevaleret*
Thursday and Sunday 8 am to 1 pm

The church of Notre Dame de la Gare in the middle of a broad plaza is the focal point of this market. What a surprise to find silver fox and mink coats on sale at one of the stands. The fish at Visery are fresh to our eyes, and our noses concur. Jean-Luc Felten, the *charcutier*, has a smile and a quip for every patron, and a line of tasty little tarts including spinach, *brioche* with sausage and pistachio, a *millefeuilles* of ham and cheese, and a *bouchée à la reine* ready to pop in the oven.

Maison-Blanche Open-Air Food Market

MARCHÉ MAISON-BLANCHE
Avenue d'Italie, from rue du Tage to
rue du Moulin de la Pointe, 13th arr.
🚇 *Maison-Blanche*
Thursday 8 am to 1:30 pm; Sunday 8 am to 2 pm

Sounds ricochet from one side to the other along this narrow sidewalk that fills with local residents, including many Chinese and Arab immigrants. Lower prices reflect the slightly lesser quality of goods, but there are gems (cheeses, eggs, fruit, meat, Polish sausages) among the bargains.

Paris Rive Gauche Open-Air Food Market

MARCHÉ PARIS RIVE GAUCHE
Enter between no. 18 and 20, rue Neuve Tolbiac, onto
rue Jean Anouilh, 13th arr.
🚇 *Bibliothèque François Mitterand*
Friday 12 pm to 8:30 pm

A few years ago this district held little more than a few ailing industrial facilities, but with the construction of the flagship Bibliothèque Nationale, a new urban zone is sprouting up. This tiny market with its handful of stalls, including one selling organic produce, is in its infancy.

Salpêtrière Open-Air Food Market

LE MARCHÉ SALPÊTRIÈRE
At the entrance to the Pitié-Salpêtrière Hospital,
boulevard de l'Hôpital, 13th arr.
🚇 *Saint-Marcel*
Tuesday and Friday 8 am to 1 pm

The métro passes overhead, and after a rainstorm the platform leaks copiously on the market below, but the architectural grandeur of the adjacent Hôpital Pitié-Salpêtriére makes the dousing worthwhile. There are vegetable stands, a fishmonger, a butcher, a *charcuterie*, and some practical clothing.

Vincent Auriol Open-Air Food Market

LE MARCHÉ VINCENT AURIOL
Boulevard Vincent Auriol from rue Jeanne d'Arc to
rue du Chevaleret, 13th arr.
🚇 *Nationale, Chevaleret*
Wednesday and Saturday 8 am to 1 pm

The columns and girders of the métro, which passes overhead with an intermittent rumble, and a row of young oak trees planted on each side, frame this market. Road traffic is noisy, but the merchants are friendly and welcoming. All the usual market stands are represented.

14TH ARRONDISSEMENT ✦ MONTPARNASSE

FOOD MARKETS

Edgar Quinet Open-Air Food Market ✦ 179

Rungis Wholesale Market ✦ 181

Mouton-Duvernet Open-Air Food Market ✦ 186
(also known as Montrouge)

Brancusi Organic Open-Air Food Market ✦ 188

Brune Open-Air Food Market ✦ 190

Rue Daguerre Market Street ✦ 191

Villemain Open-Air Food Market ✦ 192

MARKETPLACES

Edgar Quinet Arts and Crafts Market ✦ 193

Porte de Vanves Flea Market ✦ 195

Edgar Quinet Open-Air Food Market

LE MARCHÉ EDGAR QUINET
*Boulevard Edgar Quinet from rue du Départ to
square Delambre, 14th arr.*
🚇 *Edgar Quinet, Vavin*
Wednesday 8 am to 1:30 pm; Saturday 8 am to 1 pm

Behind the lively boulevard du Montparnasse—celebrated for its famous cafés—lies the calm, wooded expanse of Montparnasse cemetery on boulevard Edgar Quinet. This charming and tranquil market runs alongside it, a broad aisle with stalls on both sides along the tree-lined median plaza. At the west end, the Montparnasse tower rises like a giant tombstone. If there remains any doubt in a traveler's mind whether permitting a modern high-rise building in this part of Paris was a good idea, a visit to this market will resolve it.

In autumn we find several presentations of the ever-popular snails packed with garlic and butter (*escargots Provençale, escargots Bourguignonne*). A dozen varieties of stunningly beautiful mushrooms are laid out with pine boughs separating them: waxy *girolles*, gray *pleurottes*, orange *chanterelles*, fat brown *cèpes*, chalky white *champignons de Paris*, meaty shiitakes, oddly cleft *pied de mouton*, and somber black *trompettes de la mort*.

179

Green cabbages, sliced in half, display a Tree of Life pattern we had not noticed before. We buy pumpkin and leeks before the bins completely empty to prepare a velvety cream soup that evening. There are many examples of seasonal *charcuterie* made from ham and game, and an ever-present aroma of *choucroute*. While shopping at Teodoro, we watch a saleswoman spear a slice of bacon from the steaming pile of sauerkraut, wait for it to cool, and hand it to a boy who jumps with glee while his mother selects pâtés.

Spring offers some different choices. The scent of Gariguette strawberries perfumes the air. A much-loved French variety, their arrival at market heralds the beginning of picking season. The oblong shape makes it easy to pinch off their leafy hats and pop them directly into the mouth. Vegetables are prominent too. Maison Earl-Raehm's stand has some of the best lettuces we've seen anywhere, delivered straight from the family's farm near Paris. Eric Cazard specializes in goat cheeses and sells a few wines that best accompany them. We follow the scent of chocolate to Marie & Patrick's small homemade cakes.

Local honey is sold in plastic jars or as part of soaps, candles, and body creams. Clothing and jewelry arrive by box-loads. A man demonstrates another souvenir—special scissors for cutting fruit and vegetables. The pile of razor-thin cucumber clippings by his elbow attest to a busy morning of food artistry. Beggars and young women selling bunches of flowers often enclose this market at each end like sad parentheses. If you leave a few coins with them you'll experience a touch of grace.

Rungis Wholesale Food Market

LES HALLES DE RUNGIS
Near Orly Airport, south of the 14th arr.
No métro service
Tuesday to Sunday 2 am to 8 am
For information regarding a visit, see www.visitrungis.com

Rungis was established in 1969 when les Halles, the main food market in the center of Paris for eight centuries, was relocated outside the city. For anyone who has visited the markets and wondered where most of the food comes from, a trip to Rungis reveals the answer. It is the market behind the markets—the food wholesalers' Garden of Eden. Emile Zola's *The Belly of Paris* gives a vivid account of the original Les Halles. In the 1800s, architect Victor Baltard redesigned and enlarged Les Halles with iron and glass pavilions (see p. 139). But a century later, the market had outgrown its space in central Paris. Cramped, dirty, and rat-infested, Les Halles closed. The whole operation shifted to a new facility located seven miles south near Orly airport. The move was overseen by a WWII general experienced in large-scale troop movements in order to prevent Paris's entire food system from shutting down. It was accomplished in only two days.

One of seventeen wholesale markets in France, Rungis is by far the largest and the best. About half of its customers are retailers who sell the goods at many of the markets described in this book or in specialty shops; the remainder are restaurants and supermarkets. Staggering quantities of food move in and out quickly. Fish, we were told, travel

from the water to a fishmonger's stall within 24 hours.

Everything is gigantic: 575 acres, 45,000 square feet under roof, and more than 20,000 visitors daily, of whom about half are buyers. The markets open in the order of a French meal: the fish market at 2 am, meat at 3, vegetables and cheese at 4, and flowers last of all. In the fish and seafood hall there are big tuna, as well as crayfish, shrimp, and lobster (*les crustacées*) at one end of the hall, and shellfish (*les coquillages*) at the other. Rungis is so vast that some purchasers whiz by on bicycles while they eye the goods. Employees and buyers congregate at any of twenty on-site restaurants where they warm up from chilly conditions, negotiate deals, and—in the hallowed tradition of Les Halles— trade gossip.

The meat hall is a forest of hanging carcasses of beef, lamb, and veal; then on to the offal hall. Pork is processed in a separate building. We were somewhat prepared by our visits to the markets, but it is still a shock to see rows of pig's heads, piles of trotters, and long lines of snouts and tails. Skins from the heads are hung up like limp Halloween masks. The birds in the poultry building still have their heads on (and many their feet as well). Buyers believe this helps them judge quality and maintains freshness.

Cheeses come in 400 kinds. Huge wheels of Emmenthal and Gruyère require reinforced shelves to hold their weight. Vegetables, fruits, and flowers come from all over the world. We saw purple and yellow orchids that had just arrived from the tropics, each stem swathed in cotton to protect the delicate blooms. The flowers are so fresh they don't need to be in water. Rosebuds are curled as tight as snails and the peonies are balled like babies' fists. After so many noisy, cold halls, this one was quiet and relatively warm.

Rungis's business operations keep evolving. Buildings are constantly being added or renovated and logistics modernized. They are experimenting with online ordering and free delivery. A "producer's floor" was recently added to feature locally grown items. Several warehouses are dedicated to organic products. They are switching to a labeling system that's no longer specific to French organic products (the AB *agriculture biologique* sticker) but a common standard for the European Union. Unsold fruits and vegetables are distributed to food aid organizations rather than left to rot. Environmental efforts have been stepped up: 30,000 tons of materials are recycled annually. An on-site incinerator burns non-recyclable waste, generating enough power to heat the market plus three neighboring towns.

Few chefs come to Rungis to shop. Nowadays they rely on specialized middlemen who shop for them and deliver to their restaurants. Fax machines and the Internet have made a big difference in the way the market functions, since tradespeople don't have to stay up half the night on the telephone to place orders. The market continues to evolve in other ways. There are more prepared foods like cooked shrimp and skewered meat ready to barbecue. Improvements in distribution work in favor of small-scale merchants who buy in limited quantities.

It isn't like Les Halles, with its medieval atmosphere, wooden carts full of produce, and early morning onion soup. We feel lucky to have experienced the old market before it was moved, but we were impressed by the size and efficiency of the one that has taken its place. You can't buy anything at Rungis since trade is limited to wholesalers. But if food in all its forms interests you, as it does us, you'll want to see first-hand

how Paris and the surrounding region feed itself at such a high level of quality, day in and day out.

Tours of Rungis must be booked in advance and can be arranged via the website www.visitrungis.com. Several guides provide private tours for small groups (search the Internet). Rungis is open every day except Sunday, but the best days to visit are Tuesday, Thursday, and Friday to see all the food halls. Be prepared for an early start. Tours usually begin with the fish market around 4:30 am.

Mouton-Duvernet Open-Air Food Market

(also known as Montrouge)

LE MARCHÉ MOUTON-DUVERNET

Place Jacques Demy, bounded by rue Brézin, rue Saillard, rue Boulard,
and rue Mouton-Duvernet, 14th arr.

🚇 *Mouton-Duvernet*

Tuesday and Friday 8 am to 1:30 pm

Tucked behind busy streets, this neighborhood market provides an oasis of calm and civility. Three aisles of stands fill a small shaded square, creating a sense of abundance as well as intimacy. The friendly Crédaro family sells low-spray vegetables and field-cut flowers. Evelyne Nochet brings plums, apples, and pears from her orchard in Touraine from early fall through spring until her supply runs out. Nearby, a stand offers hot Lebanese sandwiches. The cheeses of Jean-Jacques Lainé have a country character: bits of straw and ash still cling to their rinds.

Brancusi Organic Open-Air Food Market

LE MARCHÉ BIOLOGIQUE BRANCUSI
Place Constantin Brancusi, 14th arr.
🚊 *Gaîté*
Saturday 9 am to 3 pm

The smallest of the city's three organic markets, Brancusi attracts a largely neighborhood clientele. Several sizable produce stalls offer an array of fruit and vegetables. Other friendly vendors sell fish, cheese, bread, and oysters—all crammed into a tiny but pleasant square that is surrounded by apartment buildings and anchored at one end by an organic bakery and a tea salon.

Brune Open-Air Food Market

LE MARCHÉ BRUNE

North side of Boulevard Brune, from rue Didot to rue Raymond Losserand (in front of impasse Vandal), 14th arr.

Porte de Vanves

Thursday and Sunday 8 am to 1 pm

Clothing, household goods, and a long run of vegetable and fruit stands interspersed with fishmongers, butchers, bakers, and cheese sellers make this a well-stocked market. Sausages of Jacquet de Nanterres are impressive, as well as canned quail with duck liver, *confit* of duck, and other Dordogne products. The butcher Goulet boned two rabbit haunches with the speed and precision of a cardiac surgeon. Robert Foucat has a variety of spices in small cellophane bags, ideal to take home as gifts.

Rue Daguerre Market Street

LA RUE DAGUERRE

From Avenue du Général Leclerc to rue Boulard, 14th arr.

🚇 *Denfert Rochereau*

Tuesday to Saturday 10 am to 7 pm; Sunday morning

Rue Daguerre has the friendly feel of a small village. People from the neighborhood chat while they shop, and children gather for play. Sounds of live flute and cello music floated down the pedestrian street during our Sunday visit. For gifts of foie gras and other gastronomic specialties from Périgord, check out the tins and gift baskets at Valette. Daguerre Marée piles shrimp and langoustines into great glistening pyramids, sweet to smell and good to the pocketbook. Excellent cheeses fill the case at Vacroux & Fils, a shop instantly recognizable by the large plastic replicas of cows that seem to be strolling along the balcony.

Villemain Open-Air Food Market

LE MARCHÉ VILLEMAIN

Place Lieutenant S. Piobetta, between rue d'Alésia and avenue Villemain, 14th arr.

🚇 *Plaisance*

Wednesday and Sunday 8 am to 1 pm

A typically friendly but unremarkable neighborhood market, this one comprises about twenty stands, easily accessible because of their location on two sides of a triangular garden. The produce is fresh and appealing. Michel and Christine Pérus sell pristine cheese, yogurt, and milk products.

Edgar Quinet Arts and Crafts Market

LE MARCHÉ DE LA CRÉATION EDGAR QUINET

*Median plaza of boulevard Edgar Quinet,
between rue Huyghens and rue du Départ, 14th arr.*

🚇 *Edgar Quinet*

Sunday 10 am to 7 pm

An outdoor arts and crafts market started in the 1990s in the pretty park where the Mouton-Duvernet open-air food market is located. In 1997 the artists moved to a more accessible location, in the median plaza of the boulevard Edgar Quinet, where a food market takes place twice a week. On Sunday, painters, sculptors, and a variety of craftspeople bring their work here for viewing. The art must be original, signed, and if in series not more than ten copies.

This is a market of more than a hundred artists, all looking for recognition. They are happy to talk about their work or anything else

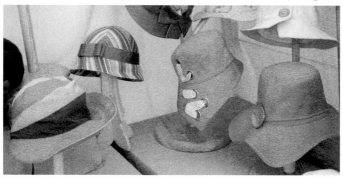

you may bring up. If the quality of the art is not up to gallery standards, much of it shows promise and all of it is ambitious. Oil and watercolor paintings intrigued us, but there are also ceramics, handmade clothing, fantasy hats, and sculpture in several media. Prices can range from ten or twenty dollars for a postcard-sized watercolor to several hundred for a large sculpture.

Some years ago we bought two oil paintings by the artist Piotrowski, each no larger than a guidebook, of the ubiquitous outdoor chairs in the Luxembourg Garden. Each arrangement of two or more empty chairs seems endowed with unique voices. All appear to be having interesting conversations with each other. We had a pleasant interaction with Eddy Panger who makes sculptures of found objects, mostly car and motorcycle parts, often using a headlight as a face. They are charming and original, but a bit too large to take home.

Serge Rat makes paintings with tiny human figures in vast, white landscapes. Something about them spoke to us. Sarah François has twisted wire into sculptures of dancers in active positions, but these too are a bit large. L. Godon makes interesting paintings of books in flight, like flocks of pigeons swooping through the sky. Next time we'll think seriously about buying one of these. Ania creates remarkable hats, usable and not too expensive. And finally, little Ella, nine years old, was offering to make our portrait in soft pencil while we waited.

Porte de Vanves Flea Market

Avenue Marc Sangnier and avenue Georges-Lafenestre, 14th arr.
🚊 *Porte de Vanves*
Saturday and Sunday 9 am to 6 pm

There is no way to easily or quickly summarize the kind or number of things for sale here. Most of it is *brocante* (bric-a-brac) but, according to a knowledgeable informant, dealers from the Clignancourt antiques and flea market shop Vanves early in the morning for overlooked bargains.

From the Vanves métro station, walk south into the place de la Porte de Vanves, then turn left onto avenue Marc Sangnier. Vanves seems to us what Clignancourt was in the old days, a vast market where the variety is as great as the price range, and where with a bit of luck you can still find good buys. The market makes an angle at the corner of avenues Sangnier and Lafenestre, with stands on both sides of the narrow side-walk under big umbrellas or makeshift covers if the weather is unfriendly. On warm days, acacia trees give protection from the sun.

Much of what we see appears to be from the twentieth century: glassware, table settings, ashtrays, furniture, and a large assortment of *bandes dessinées* or hardcover comic books. What might we take home with us? Vintage glassware,

asparagus and oyster platters, old linens, silver-plated tableware, art deco vases, corkscrews made from dried grapevines—the list is endless.

We've looked for crystal champagne flutes in every flea market and antique shop we've visited, and Vanves does not disappoint. But there's much more: Art Nouveau objects such as coffee-table sculptures and champagne buckets, along with the furniture that was popular between the World Wars, and classical pieces such as armoires, bedside tables, and *tables de ferme* (farmhouse tables). With luck, you might even find an old *garde-manger*, a wooden cage that hung in a cool place near the kitchen to keep leftovers, cheeses, and vegetables.

A visit to a flea market is a bit like peering in the windows of elderly neighbors who are about to move into a retirement home. They've

kept everything from their marriages and their visits to foreign countries. Vanished passions are displayed like outgrown clothing, whether ceramic jugs or African wood carvings. Family traditions are displayed too: linen napkins with embroidered initials of grandparents, and table settings handed down from one or more families. One can't help feeling a bit like a peeping Tom, yet one can't help looking.

You can spend half an hour in the Vanves flea market, or half a day with a lunch break at the Café Didot at the intersection of the avenues Sangnier and Lafenestre. Or you can walk up to the boulevard Brune on Sunday and gather the makings of a picnic in the open-air food market there. If a ham sandwich is enough to soothe the savage beast, food stands located throughout the market will provide it. There may be a soccer game underway on the adjacent field. There's a lot to see, a lot to think about, and perhaps even a purchase to make before leaving.

15TH ARRONDISSEMENT · VAUGIRARD

FOOD MARKETS

Grenelle Open-Air Food Market · 201

Brassens Open-Air Food Market · 203

Cervantes Open-Air Food Market · 203

Convention Open-Air Food Market · 204

Covered Fish Market – Samurais of the Seas · 205

Lecourbe Open-Air Food Market · 208

Lefevbre Open-Air Food Market · 208

Saint-Charles Open-Air Food Market · 209

MARKETPLACES

Antiquarian and Used Book Market · 211

Grenelle Open-Air Food Market

LE MARCHÉ GRENELLE
*Boulevard de Grenelle from rue de Lourmel to
rue du Commerce, 15th arr.*
🚇 *Dupleix, La Motte-Picquet Grenelle*
Wednesday 8 am to 1:30 pm; Sunday 8 am to 2 pm

Below the train tracks of La Motte-Piquet Grenelle lies an exciting underworld of commerce. Colorful scarves swirl from hangers at stalls around the edges. Step onto the wide walkway and discover all kinds of food, basic housewares, jewelry, and clothing arranged in orderly displays. At Marc's produce stand, leeks fan out like perfectly spaced chorus dancers, and radishes point their white toes upward. Evelyne Nochet brings fruits from her Loire orchard, including over forty varieties of apples and eight of pears that rotate in and out as their growing seasons permit. In August and September, she sells the famed Reine Claude plums. They were named for the wife of François I who adored them, and proclaimed by food blogger David Lebovitz as "perhaps the most delicious fruit in the world."

A few stalls down, the mushroom enthusiast Bouclet shares his beau-

tiful shiitakes, oyster mushrooms (*pleurotes*), golden chanterelles, and large *eryngii* (also known as King Oyster or King Trumpet). He'll gladly explain how their flavors compare and how to use them in cooking. For cheeses, La Ferme du Poirier Rond from Saint-Vrain does a brisk business. The owner, Philippe Perette, personally tastes and selects the wheels of cheese he sells each week and clearly has a discriminating palate. His goat's milk, ewe, and cow cheeses can be relied upon for their consistent and exceptional quality. For eggs, David Brocker's stand offers a good variety.

Although frequented almost exclusively by locals, a savvy tourist would do well to wind up in this marvelous market, especially on a Sunday.

Brassens Open-Air Food Market

LE MARCHÉ BRASSENS

*Place Jacques Marette, at the intersection of rue des Morillons and
rue Cronstadt, 15th arr.*

🚇 *Porte de Vanves, Convention*

Friday 3 pm to 8:30 pm

This tiny market is open on Friday afternoons, giving those in the
neighborhood a chance to pick up provisions on their way home from
work. Like some of the other afternoon markets, Brassens seems to be
struggling. Choices are limited and there's only a trickle of customers. It
feels more like a glorified fruit stand than a thriving market.

Cervantes Open-Air Food Market

LE MARCHÉ CERVANTES

Place Wassily Kandinsky, opposite nos. 49-51, rue Bargue, 15th arr.

🚇 *Volontaires*

Wednesday and Saturday 8 am to 1 pm

High-rise apartment buildings tower over this market. The location is
somewhat colorless, but the market has personality, perhaps because of
the friendliness of vendors unaccustomed to visitors from a distant part
of Paris. Half the market is under an arcade, important if the day is cold
and drizzly.

Convention Open-Air Food Market

LE MARCHÉ CONVENTION
*Rue de la Convention from rue de Vaugirard to
place Charles Vallin, 15th arr.*
🚇 *Convention*
Tuesday and Thursday 8 am to 1:30 pm; Sunday 8 am to 2 pm

This enormous market runs along both sides of rue de la Convention. It's one of the more difficult markets to navigate. Shoppers squeeze past each other on the narrow sidewalk. But pleasant interactions and a broad selection create a convivial atmosphere. A large quantity of meat, fish, poultry, produce—as well as cosmetics, DVDs, and clothing—move from merchants' tables to shoppers' baskets in a spirit of good-humored haggling. Maison Lenoble's salad greens come straight from the farm in Perigny. The fish at Les Maisons de l'Océan rest on beds of ice tucked inside wicker baskets. Several stalls away, Pierre Reininger

is the fourth generation in his family's spice business. Mixtures sealed in plastic pouches make inexpensive gifts that are easy to carry.

Covered Fish Market—Samurais of the Seas

HALLE AUX POISSONS-LES SAMOURAÏS DES MERS
69, rue Castagnary at rue des Morillons, 15th arr.
🚃 *Plaisance*
Tuesday to Saturday 9 am to 9 pm; Sunday 9 am to 7 pm

This emporium surfaces in an unlikely place and takes some effort to find, but for fish lovers it's like discovering buried treasure. If you approach from the south, a white and red lighthouse and a painted sailor standing in the bow of a nearly life-sized Breton fishing boat are moored in the ridge overhead. Neon letters used to spell out *Gloire à nos marins pecheurs* (Glory to our fishermen on the sea) but they're deteriorating badly. Nestled next to the train tracks, this icon provides reassurance that you're in the right place no matter how incongruous the scene may look.

Inside, the décor is just as quirky—pure kitsch enlivened with bright lights, painted scenes, a Santa Claus, a fairy castle, and the best selection of fish we've found anywhere in Paris. Unlike other markets that include multiple stalls, Samurais of the Seas is one big outlet managed by a single owner who caters to both retail and wholesale clients.

205

Many of the fish we admired were line-caught and delivered fresh off small boats at 4 am that morning. Other catches looked as fresh but had traveled farther: mackerel, anchovies, and sardines as silvery as polished knife blades; fiery red scorpion fish (*rascasse*) ablaze atop crushed ice; pearl-white sea bream with a rosy blush of pink-tipped fins; and John Dory with golden mouths agape and fins like fringed hems of fine drapery. In the rear, a *halle aux huîtres et crustacés* is devoted to oysters and other shellfish such as mussels, crabs, lobsters, and shrimp, live or cooked.

A child could practice ABCs with the veritable alphabet of well-labeled fish. We picked out a single filet of lemon sole while another customer purchased multiple kilos for his restaurant. Shelves well stocked with wines that best accompany the fish as well as tins of foie gras (for taking home in your suitcase), smoked salmon, and other specialty foods practically enable one-stop shopping for dinner. Platters can be made to order as well. With discounted pricing, excellent quality, and a selection as wide as an estuary, it's a wonder that even more shoppers weren't swimming in the doors.

Lecourbe Open-Air Food Market

LE MARCHÉ LECOURBE
Rue Lecourbe from rue Leblanc to rue Vasco de Gama, 15th arr.
🚊 *Balard, Lourmel*
Wednesday and Saturday 8 am to 1 pm

In this distant corner of the city, activity speeds up after midday to dispose of remaining produce. Vendors call out bargains, improving the terms as one o'clock approaches. One day we saw cantaloupe prices drop like rocks. At the last minute, shoppers stagger off with cartons of salad greens or tomatoes for the equivalent of a dollar or less.

Lefevbre Open-Air Food Market

LE MARCHÉ LEFEVBRE
Boulevard Lefevbre between rue de Dantzig and
rue Olivier de Serres, 15th arr.
🚊 *Porte de Versailles*
Wednesday and Saturday 8 am to 1 pm

Sidewalks are the most common location for small markets like this one. All the usual stalls are here to supply the neighborhood. At Le Callebasse, a pair of African women sometimes sell unusual cocktail hors d'oeuvres.

Saint-Charles Open-Air Food Market

LE MARCHÉ SAINT-CHARLES
Rue Saint-Charles, from rue de Javel to rue des Cévennes, 15th arr.
🚊 *Charles Michels*
Tuesday and Friday 8 am to 1 pm

Sycamores give some shade to this narrow, one-way street. The east side is given almost exclusively to food stalls, while the west side, from rue de la Convention to rue des Cévennes, is mostly clothing. We discovered Sylvain Hordesseaux, whose seasonal rhubarb and asparagus are garden-fresh, along with carrots, onions, radishes, and other good things.

Antiquarian and Used Book Market

LE MARCHÉ DU LIVRE ANCIEN ET D'OCCASION
Parc Georges Brassens, rue Brancion, 15th arr.
🚇 *Porte de Vanves, Convention*
Saturday and Sunday 9 am to 6 pm

This market is located in two open-air pavilions surrounded by a handsome iron fence. A tile roof floats on cast iron pillars over tables laden with books of every description—old, valuable, rare, and unique. Seventy to one hundred vendors come here every weekend, depending on the season and the weather. Goods range from magazines and books of photography to scholarly tomes, hardcover and softcover, some current and some long out of date. Many are spread out side-by-side on trestle tables so their titles and contents can easily be seen. Others are presented in boxes, piled neatly or stacked carelessly, according to the whim and style of the seller.

The market is divided into two parts linked by an open courtyard. Standing on the brick pavers is a larger-than-life bronze sculpture of a butcher with half a carcass across his shoulders, testimony to the slaughterhouse that once occupied this space. As with other structures inspired by nineteenth-century tastes, the airy feeling here might have been created by spiders working in iron, glass, and tile. Lighted globes hang in the arches, and on cold, gloomy days neon tubes give the space a uniform brightness.

Studious, well-dressed clients browse or search for particular items; some chat quietly with the vendors, encouraging a love of books in the well-behaved children they've brought with them. Like the children, we were drawn to the *bandes-dessinées*, comic books between hard covers such as the adventures of Tintin, Asterix, Lucky Luke, and others. But the business of this market is mainly biography, history, novels, poems, and plays. It's one of the few places where we've seen old 33 $\frac{1}{3}$ rpm records in their original sleeves. When all is said and done, this is one of the calmest, loveliest, and most serious of all the markets of Paris.

It's worth stepping into the adjacent Georges Brassens Park, on the site that was once the Vaugirard slaughterhouse. Horses were auctioned here right into the mid-twentieth century. Now, paths wind through gently sculptured topography furnished with ponds, play structures, and outdoor sculptures. There are joggers and strollers, and a few young women in bikinis stretched out under the sun on a small green lawn. Among other interesting features are a scent garden for the blind, a bee-keeping school, a small vineyard, and a marionette theater.

16TH ARRONDISSEMENT • TROCADÉRO

FOOD MARKETS

Président Wilson Open-Air Food Market • 215

In Search of Superior Taste • 218

Amiral Bruix Open-Air Food Market • 220

Auteuil Open-Air Food Market • 220

Gros-la-Fontaine Open-Air Food Market • 221

Passy Covered Food Market • 222

Point du Jour Open-Air Food Market • 222

Porte Molitor Open-Air Food Market • 223

Rue de l'Annonciation Market Street • 223

Saint-Didier Covered Food Market • 224

MARKETPLACES

Auteuil Antiques Village • 224

Président Wilson Open-Air Food Market

LE MARCHÉ PRÉSIDENT WILSON

Avenue du Président Wilson from
place d'Iéna to rue Debrousse, 16th arr.

🚇 *Iéna*

Wednesday 8 am to 1:30 pm; Saturday 8 am to 2 pm

This marvelous open market starts at the place d'Iéna near the striking sculpture of George Washington on horseback, his sword raised high, and stretches for several blocks along a slight slope. The wide boulevard is shaded by acacia trees and is home to handsome residential buildings with graceful Mansard roofs and wrought-iron balconies. A visit here can be combined with sightseeing at the Palais de Tokyo with its ever-changing avant-garde art exhibits; the Musée d'Art Moderne de la Ville de Paris next door; or the Musée Galliera (fashion museum) across the street. All are clustered at the midpoint of the market stalls.

The aromas will draw you in. Tantalizing perfumes of lilies, tulips, and roses waft from the flower stands. At Crêperie Bretonne, Gerard pours batter onto hot griddles to make sweet crêpes and savory *galettes de sarrasin* from buckwheat flour, such as the Celtique which is spread with

cheese, onions, and andouille sausage. A line forms as lunchtime approaches, and customers take seats at a makeshift table. Several rotisserie stands tempt with perfectly browned chicken which they'll slip into a bag to send home warm.

The Thiébault family has operated a market stand since 1873 (originally at another Paris location), bringing vegetables grown on their land in Carrières-sur-Seine. Joël Thiébault has taken the family business to new heights by specializing in unusual and heirloom varieties (see In Search of Superior Taste, p. 213). Savvy customers, including some of the city's top chefs, arrive early for the best pick.

Make a sweep through the entire market before deciding what and where to buy. Stalls abound with fresh produce, including one devoted to organic. Fishmongers practically compete for the most eye-catching displays. Poissonnerie Lorenzo is one of our favorites. Schools of fish, their skins glistening all the pink and silvery hues of the sea, seem to swim in parallel formation atop ice.

A superb selection of mushrooms and herbs arrayed in baskets

awaits at Bar à Patates. Nearby, fresh ravioli stuffed with chèvre or spinach and walnuts at a booth selling Italian specialties go fast. Monsieur Marc arranges *pâtisseries artisanale* that were baked early the same morning, including a flan with cherries. Crisscrossed loaves of golden breads, many still warm, prove irresistible. Another stand sells dried fruits, nuts, olives, and marinated anchovies.

Many different gifts can be purchased here, from reasonably priced jewelry, clothing, and handbags, to bagfuls of sea salt and tins of foie gras made from duck liver and the creamier tasting (and more expensive) goose liver pâté. Toward closing time, some vendors speed sales by steeply discounting their prices and calling out to passers-by: "*Je finis la table, venez faire le choix!*" (I'm clearing the table, so come and make your choice.) But personally we prefer to arrive early while the stands are full of artistically displayed produce, as fresh and tempting as we have seen anywhere.

We were dizzied by the number of opportunities to buy fruits and vegetables when we started shopping at neighborhood markets in Paris. Most merchants present comparable selections, which will vary by season, but it can be difficult to identify those who offer anything truly special. Over time we noticed differences and began identifying a few vendors whom we now seek out for their exceptional quality. One way to target preferred vendors is painfully obvious: Look where the locals wait in queues. Take your place in line and pass the time by observing what they buy. Another is to look for signage that promotes a seller's direct connection to the land. Some of our favorites are *maraîchers* or *producteurs*, who grow their own and sell without any middlemen. Evelyne Nochet's apples, pears, and plums from her own orchard are

in a class of their own; so too are Earl Raehm's salad greens and others whose stands are mentioned in these pages.

Discerning cooks make a beeline to Joël Thiébault's stand at Marché Président Wilson and Marché Gros-La-Fontaine in the 16th arrondissement, often first thing in the morning for the best pick. We once arrived at opening and saw a chef in his white uniform selecting vegetables (touching and smelling them in ways we would never dare) and filling several bins for that day's menu.

Thiébault's passion is cultivating unusual and almost extinct varieties that are packed full of flavor. He exchanges seeds with farmers around the world. During one visit we could choose from six types of potatoes. Some were small, black, and gnarly. Others golden and red-speckled. For carrots, no fewer than five varieties—and none of them the standard orange. Each is identified with a sign and poetic description. Le Chantenay carrots have *une forte personalité*, while Yellow Stones stand out for *un doux parfum puissant*, and the curvy Parmex is une *parisienne toute en rondeur*. Come tomato season, Thiébault's stand overflows with heirloom varieties, each boasting a unique taste. He grows sixty types of tomatoes but has experimented with over a hundred.

Joël Thiébault's vegetables come from Carrières-sur-Seine. He told us that his family has been farming this land since the Middle Ages! A typical day starts at 4 am. He reviews what's freshest, assembles orders, and decides what will go on the truck for market days. The phone rings early with calls from some of the city's best restaurants. His clientele has among them more stars than the Cassiopeia constellation. But Thiébault has not lost direct contact with the day-to-day open markets where loyal shoppers give him feedback on what they like or don't. A knowledgeable team of farmhands helps assist shoppers since Thiébault is often called away to the phone to take special orders or to consult his computer which lies open on the truck floor atop gritty soil that shook off that morning's haul of fresh-picked winners.

Amiral Bruix Open-Air Food Market

LE MARCHÉ AMIRAL BRUIX
Boulevard de l'Amiral Bruix, from rue Weber to rue Marbeau, 16th arr.
🚇 *Porte Maillot*
Wednesday and Saturday 8 am to 1 pm

This small market does a local business at a leisurely pace, in a pretty setting in the northwest corner of the 16th arrondissement. A poultry vendor, working behind a small screen, prepared a duckling for a customer by burning off the pinfeathers with a small gas torch.

Auteuil Open-Air Food Market

LE MARCHÉ AUTEUIL
Place Jean Lorrain, 16th arr.
🚇 *Michel-Ange Auteuil*
Wednesday 8 am to 1:30 pm; Saturday 8 am to 2 pm

This delightful little square is packed full of stalls on market days. Except for the narrow aisles, every centimeter seems to be claimed. Some stands spill over the edges with an occasional potato or strawberry rolling into the street. Discriminating shoppers abound—locals mostly, since few tourists venture out this far. The vendors' standards meet their discerning customers' expectations. Sausages hang from the canopy at Boucherie Felz, fish glisten atop ice at Poissonnerie Barret, and rotisserie chickens are sold at Priolet Artisan Volailler.

Gros-la-Fontaine Open-Air Food Market

LE MARCHÉ GROS-LA-FONTAINE

Rue Gros from rue Gautier to rue Jean de la Fontaine, and
rue Jean de la Fontaine from rue Gros to rue de Boulainvilliers, 16th arr.

🚇 *Jasmin, Ranelagh*

Tuesday and Friday 8 am to 1:30 pm

This pleasant L-shaped market emerges where rue Gros intersects rue Jean de la Fontaine at the shady square du Pré aux Chevaux, or Horse Pasture Square. The market reflects the arrondissement in the high quality and fastidious displays. Stroll down rue Clos to find flower stands, fishmongers, cheeses, and certified organic produce. Bins of oysters have been brought in fresh from Charente-Maritime. One stand sells *manoush*, a Lebanese-style pizza made with thyme-sprinkled dough, heated on a griddle, and slathered with hummus, tabouli, or falafel for an eat-on-the-spot treat. Joël Thiébault (see p. 218) brings his uncommon varieties of vegetables, and the best items sell out early. More food and clothing stalls extend along the other limb of the market.

Passy Covered Food Market

LE MARCHÉ COUVERT PASSY
1, rue Bois le Vent, place de Passy at the corner of rue Duban, 16th arr.
🚇 *La Muette*
Tuesday to Saturday 8 am to 1 pm, 4 pm to 7 pm;
Sunday 8 am to 1 pm

The anonymous concrete façade of this building may be off-putting, but a glass brick skylight and windows make the interior bright and airy. The Carioti family sells dried and fresh pastas, and raviolis stuffed with Gorgonzola, chopped ham, and other combinations. Le Boulanger du Marché has fresh-baked country-style breads from a wood-fired oven, including a five-grain loaf and a sunflower-seed variation known as a *polka*.

Point du Jour Open-Air Food Market

LE MARCHÉ POINT DU JOUR
Avenue de Versailles from rue Gudin to rue le Marois, 16th arr.
🚇 *Porte de Saint-Cloud*
Tuesday and Thursday 8 am to 1:30 pm; Sunday 8 am to 2 pm

A row of stalls along the east side of the avenue expands into three aisles filling the place du Président Paul Reynaud. It would be hard to find more flawless berries, melons, or peaches than those sold here, or thicker spears of white asparagus that appear for only a few weeks in early spring.

Porte Molitor Open-Air Food Market

LE MARCHÉ PORTE MOLITOR

Place de la Porte Molitor from avenue du Général Sarrail to boulevard Murat, 16th arr.

🚇 *Michel-Ange Molitor, Porte d'Auteuil*

Tuesday and Friday 8 am to 1:30 pm

A small market in a quiet residential neighborhood, its special attraction is the proximity to the Jardin des Serres d'Auteuil botanical gardens at the southern edge of the Bois de Boulogne. If you want to fill a picnic basket, this market has the provisions. Stock up on grape leaves and tabouli, chèvre wrapped in speck, mushrooms marinated in olive oil, a wedge of *brie de Meaux*, and a loaf of bread. Add a bunch of grapes and a bottle of wine, and you'll feast like the royalty who used to frequent the nearby hunting grounds.

Rue de l'Annonciation Market Street

RUE DE L'ANNONCIATION

Place de Passy to rue Lekain, 16th arr.

🚇 *La Muette*

Tuesday and Saturday 10 am to 6 pm; Sunday morning

A small street market cannot easily be charming and do its job, but this one handles both and, though it is one of the shortest market streets in Paris, has all the necessary food, wine, and flower shops.

Saint-Didier Covered Food Market

LE MARCHÉ COUVERT SAINT-DIDIER
Corner of rue Saint-Didier and rue Mesnil, 16th arr.
🚇 *Victor-Hugo, Boissière*
Tuesday, Thursday, Friday, and
Saturday 8:30 am to 1 pm for the market; 4 pm to 7:30 pm for the shops

From the outside, this market looks like a reduced version of a mid-nineteenth century Baltard-style building. Inside, it is small and lacks any product or service of note. Outside on the rue Mesnil, a dozen open-air stands provide fresh meat, fish, poultry, and vegetables.

Auteuil Antiques Village

HALLE D'AUTEUIL
13, rue Théophile Gautier, 16th arr.
🚇 *Église d'Auteuil*
Daily except Monday 10 am to 6 pm;
some shops close from noon to 2 pm or later

Eight or ten antique shops surround a small tearoom and restaurant. Considering the upscale character of the neighborhood, treasure may lurk here undiscovered.

17TH ARRONDISSEMENT • BATIGNOLLES

FOOD MARKETS

Batignolles Covered Food Market • 2 2 6

Batignolles Organic Open-Air Food Market • 2 2 6

Berthier Open-Air Food Market • 2 2 7

Navier Open-Air Food Market • 2 2 7

Ternes Covered Food Market • 2 2 8

Rue de Lévis Market Street • 2 2 9

Rue Poncelet Market Street • 2 2 9

MARKETPLACES

Place des Ternes Flower Market • 2 3 0

Batignolles Covered Food Market

LE MARCHÉ COUVERT BATIGNOLLES
96 bis, rue Lemercier, 17th arr.
🚇 *Brochant, Fourche*
Tuesday to Saturday 8 am to 12:30 pm, 4 pm to 7:30 pm;
Sunday 8 am to 12:45 pm

Batignolles has suffered the fate of several other covered markets. Its Baltard-style building was replaced in 1979 by an ugly concrete structure whose ground floor serves as a market. Nevertheless, the sellers are friendly and accommodating. An advertisement for free-range Brittany hogs catches our eye: "*Chez nous, être cochon c'est naturel,*" which we translate as "With us, being a pig is natural."

Batignolles Organic Open-Air Food Market

LE MARCHÉ BIOLOGIQUE DES BATIGNOLLES
Boulevard des Batignolles from rue de Turin to
rue de Moscou, 8th and 17th arr.
🚇 *Rome, Place de Clichy*
Saturday 8 am to 2 pm

See complete description in the 8th arrondissement, p. 105.

Berthier Open-Air Food Market

LE MARCHÉ BERTHIER
Boulevard de Reims beside the square A. Ulmann,
from rue du Marquis d'Arlandes to rue de Senlis, 17th arr.
🚇 *Porte de Champerret*
Wednesday and Saturday 8 am to 1 pm

A neighborhood market at the very edge of the *périphérique*—standard offerings of meat, fish, poultry, fruit, vegetables, and cheese, sold by agreeable vendors.

Navier Open-Air Food Market

LE MARCHÉ NAVIER
Rue Navier behind the church of St. Joseph-des-Épinettes, 17th arr.
🚇 *Porte de Saint-Ouen, Guy Môquet*
Tuesday and Friday 8 am to 1 pm

This is a quiet neighborhood of small apartment buildings. Across the street from the tiny market the local restaurant-bar, La Pétanque, seems to have been lifted from a village in rural France. The market and the bar, along with the nearby school and the cemetery, present enduring characteristics of French life.

Ternes Covered Food Market

LE MARCHÉ COUVERT TERNES
8 bis, rue Lebon, in the block bounded by rue Toricelli, rue Faraday,
rue Lebon, and rue Bayen, 17th arr.
🚇 *Ternes*
Tuesday to Saturday 7:30 am to 1:30 pm, 4 pm to 7 pm;
Sunday 7:30 am to 1 pm

The Baltard-style 1852 market pavilion was torn down, to re-emerge in 1970 in a radically different form. Were it not for the yellow and green sign hanging over the entrance, you might miss this market entirely. A dry-cleaning and clothing repair shop are featured. The flowers, fish, and cheese look and smell splendid, and there is plenty from which to choose. A small bakery is a pleasant addition, and the coffee shop features a variety of fresh grinds and a selection of loose teas.

Rue de Lévis Market Street

LA RUE DE LÉVIS
Between rue Legendre and place P. Goubaux, 17th arr.
🚇 *Villiers*
Tuesday to Saturday 10 am to 6 pm; Sunday morning

A long pedestrian street, rue de Lévis offers a mixture of food, clothing, flowers, and services. Though not particularly colorful, it serves its neighborhood with a full complement of specialized shops and two Monoprix supermarkets.

Rue Poncelet Market Street

LA RUE PONCELET
From avenue des Ternes to rue Bayen, 17th arr.
🚇 *Place des Ternes*
Tuesday to Saturday 10 am to 6 pm; Sunday morning

A few blocks west of place des Ternes, this fine neighborhood market sits on the angle formed by rue Bayen and rue Poncelet. The big shop at the corner, Boucheries Roger, forms the hinge. There are good fishmongers and produce stands in both streets. Two *stübli* in rue Poncelet advertise German-Austrian pastries and East European specialties.

Place des Ternes Flower Market

LE MARCHÉ AUX FLEURS TERNES
Center of place des Ternes, 17th arr.
🚇 *Ternes*
Tuesday to Sunday 8 am to 7:30 pm

Four aging plywood buildings with roofs half glass and half corrugated metal house a variety of flowers and plants, though nothing quite so spectacular as the flower market on the Île de la Cité. The advantages are that it serves a large part of the city for which the main flower market would be distant and difficult, and that it stays open long hours. After a visit and a chat with the caretakers, we felt some uncertainty about the posted hours.

18TH ARRONDISSEMENT · MONTMARTRE

FOOD MARKETS

Barbès Open-Air Food Market · 233

La Chapelle Covered Food Market · 237

Ney Open-Air Food Market · 239

Ordener Open-Air Food Market · 240

Ornano Open-Air Food Market · 240

Rue Dejean Market Street · 241

Rue du Poteau-Rue Duhesme Market Street · 242

MARKETPLACES

Clignancourt Flea Market · 243

Brocante Fairs · 246

Saint-Pierre Fabric Market · 247

Barbès Open-Air Food Market

LE MARCHÉ BARBÈS

Boulevard de la Chapelle from rue Guy Patin to
rue de Tombouctou, 18th arr.

🚇 *Barbès-Rochechouart*

Wednesday 8 am to 1:30 pm; Saturday 8 am to 2 pm

Numerous nationalities converge in this section of the 18th arrondissement known as la Goutte d'Or (or "Drop of Gold," a reference to the vineyards that used to cover the sunny slopes). Although not far in distance, Marché Barbès is leagues away in atmosphere from the heavily touristed sites of Sacré Coeur and Montmartre. Here, Muslim women in full-length black burkas move elbow-to-elbow with women from northern and western Africa wrapped in dazzling colored dresses as they each buy their weekly provisions. Men gather in eddies of conversation off to the sides. Shoppers pour onto the walkway under the train trestle, surging for-ward as if in one big wave. Looking down on the scene from the height of the métro stairs, it's a breathtaking sight—a sea of bobbing heads with patches of blue canvas stretched like rafts over stalls.

Even the smells come in surges: fresh mint, chives,

coriander, parsley, and then pungent odors of fish, aromatic spices, and sharp-smelling cheeses. Meats are hard to find since the area is primarily Muslim and butchers who abide by the Halal methods of slaughtering animals have claimed the corners of the surrounding neighborhood. Instead, the emphasis here is on vegetables, fruits, and spices, and herbs common in African and Arab cuisines. One of the many herb sellers fashions sprigs of bay leaves into a small broom to sweep stray parsley droppings from his counter.

Vendors shout *"allez-y, allez goutez!"* (come on, come taste) and extend samples of juicy orange on the tips of their knives. Others cry *"un euro, un euro!"* as they entice with bargain prices. The train rumbles overhead and voices rise to be heard. Some tourists, bombarded by sensory overload, dash into a gap between stalls to catch a moment of relative calm.

Shoppers look for bargains, and they are everywhere to be found. Vegetables and fruits are inexpensive, with the best deals for several kilos. Many customers sweep up bagfuls without concern for quality. Others are more discriminating, turning the apples and tomatoes to inspect for bruises. But no one dallies for long, neither the buyers nor the sellers. Decisions are made quickly and purchases completed briskly amid the fast flow of commerce.

Piles of fresh bell peppers, eggplants, carrots, and leeks get picked through and then replenished. Heaps of pears and lemons compete for space with mottled melons. Emptied crates are tossed to the side. A rogue fennel bulb bounces off a stand, gets kicked along and squashed underfoot. Stray lettuce leaves and discarded fruit peels litter the walkway like tossed confetti.

Stalls of clothing and fabric line the ends of the market. Red, green, and gold embroidered dresses shimmer like rainbows in the morning sun. Displays of hanging pajamas inflate with the breeze, like sleepwalkers about to set off. Shoppers rummage through bins of underclothes, shaking the items and checking for size.

We enjoy Marché Barbès mostly for the sheer exhilaration of diving headfirst into the swirling market activity. But it's not for the faint-hearted. We saw a daring beggar on the ground with a bucket for change between his folded legs—a wonder that he didn't get trampled. Pickpockets sometimes lurk among the pressing throng. Expect to be jostled, and your toes to be bumped by shoppers' carts. It's all part of the experience. As you leave the market, the din recedes but the memories linger. You might, like us, even miss it.

La Chapelle Covered Food Market

LE MARCHÉ COUVERT LA CHAPELLE
10, rue l'Olive, 18th arr.
🚇 *Marx-Dormoy*
Tuesday to Saturday 9 am to 1 pm, 4 pm to 7:30 pm;
Sunday 8:30 am to 1 pm

This might be the finest covered market still functioning in all of Paris. The vendors offer quality items and a good selection, but the main attraction is the building itself. Commonly known as "Marché de l'Olive," this splendid specimen of Baltard architecture (see p. 139) dates back to 1885 and reopened in September 2010 after 2½ years of renovations. It looks like no expense was spared in returning the building to its former glory.

The project planners showed great respect by preserving the architectural elements that gave the original design its distinction. The building proudly sits at the center of a paved pedestrian plaza just off the main boulevard, Marx-Dormoy. Its exterior walls are covered with pale orange mortar, divided into large rectangles separated by iron framing. Step inside, and that's where the design really excites. The soaring ceiling, lacy cast-iron supports, tall columns, and spacious corridors make Marché La Chapelle feel, indeed, like an inviting chapel. A glass light well runs almost the full length of the pavilion roof, permitting natural light to stream in and illuminate the farthest reaches. The grand scale of the wide open overhead spaces gets reduced to equally well-thought-out details at eye level. Individual stalls have been completely refur-

bished. Silvery metal mesh curtains serve as partitions. Counters shine, and translucent overhangs directly above each stall provide maximum light and echo the larger design. Even the gray floor tiles look and feel good underfoot.

There are excellent cheese shops, and all the other typical market fare of quality meats, fruits, and vegetables can be easily procured. Sausages and pâtés are well-displayed. Friendly merchants seem happy to be doing business in such a grand space. (They had been displaced to stalls outside during the long renovation process.) Several eateries offer sitting areas. A Moroccan *traiteur*, or delicatessen, sells steaming pots of couscous and reminds us that we're located in a vibrant ethnic enclave in this northeastern Paris neighborhood. Whether coming for the food, the architecture, or both, visitors who venture here will be duly rewarded.

Ney Open-Air Food Market

LE MARCHÉ NEY

From rue Camille Flammarion to rue Jean Varenne, 18th arr.

🚇 *Porte de Clignancourt, Porte de Saint-Ouen*

Thursday and Sunday 8:30 am to 1:30 pm

This relatively new market has quickly become popular with local residents. Beginning with a row of food stalls, it's vegetables and more vegetables, fruit, a fish seller and, on the spur going up Porte de Montmartre, handbags, clothing, shoes, and the like. Off to the side are the usual purveyors of CDs and other gadgets, but fewer than in other markets. The cries of vendors rise above the hubbub of the crowd: "*ananas, ananas*" (pineapples) and "*ooh, la la, un euro.*" Whatever it may be, it seems it can be had for one euro.

Ordener Open-Air Food Market

LE MARCHÉ ORDENER

Rue Ordener from rue Montcalm to rue Championnet, 18th arr.

🚇 *Guy Moquet, Jules Joffrin*

Wednesday and Saturday 8 am to 1 pm

The market is on a narrow sidewalk, so shoppers are squeezed between the stalls and the shops, most of which stay open on market days. One of our favorite *charcuteries*, Joelle et Elivette, is here, as well as Atlan, a fruit and vegetable stand with a good selection and competitive prices.

Ornano Open-Air Food Market

LE MARCHÉ ORNANO

*Boulevard Ornano, between rue du Mont Cenis and
rue Ordener, 18th arr.*

🚇 *Simplon*

Tuesday, Friday, and Sunday 8 am to 1 pm

Though only a short walk from the city hall and the rue Duhesme street market, the Ornano open market seems quite different in character and clientele. Most sellers and buyers are North African, and the goods reflect their tastes: heaps of dried spices, bunches of fresh mint, and cuts of lamb and kid.

Rue Dejean Market Street

LA RUE DEJEAN

Between rue Poulet and rue des Poissonniers, 18th arr.

🚇 *Chateau Rouge*

Tuesday to Saturday 10 am to 6 pm; Sunday morning

This short street behind the Gare du Nord is in a sub-Saharan African neighborhood. The butcher shops feature cuts of goat and mutton that appeal to local residents. The produce stands have more than the ordinary percentage of bruised fruits and vegetables. Most shoppers bargain vigorously, and there is a good-natured hubbub throughout the day. As the closing hour approaches, remainders are hawked at rock-bottom prices.

Rue du Poteau-Rue Duhesme Market Street

LA RUE DU POTEAU-RUE DUHESME
From rue du Poteau at place Charles Bernard to rue Ordener, 18th arr.
🚇 *Jules Joffrin*
Tuesday to Saturday 10 am to 6 pm; Sunday morning

In the rue du Poteau look for Maistre Guillaume, who spit-roasts everything in huge brick ovens: whole chickens, turkey thighs, quail, ducks, rabbits, spareribs, and boned turkey roasts stuffed with prunes or chestnuts, or wrapped with bacon. White-coated employees pull off the roasted ribs, joints, or birds, and put them into foil-lined paper bags with a little juice. Farther on, the tiny rue Duhesme, no more than ten shop-fronts in length, packs in all the essential goods and services of a typical market street. Fine vegetables are well displayed, along with fresh and diverse offerings of fish and shellfish, a neat, clean butcher shop, a proper bakery, and a *charcuterie*.

Clignancourt Flea Market

LE MARCHÉ AUX PUCES DE SAINT-OUEN/CLIGNANCOURT
Porte de Clignancourt, adjacent to the 18th arr.
🚇 *Porte de Clignancourt*
Saturday 9 am to 6 pm; Sunday 10 am to 6 pm; Monday 11 am to 5 pm
Official website: www.parispuces.com

Everyone has heard about the enormous flea market just outside Paris. The French call it les Puces de Saint-Ouen, or les Puces de Clignancourt, referring to the métro stop and *périphérique* entrance/exit here. Though it's called a flea market, Clignancourt has evolved into an antiques market with a very large number of specialists, as well as generalists who offer everything from period armchairs to World War II aircraft parts. On our first visit many years ago, this market was a dusty field with randomly parked trucks and wobbly trestle tables. But time changes all things.

From the Porte de Clignancourt métro station, walk north along the boulevard Porte de Clignancourt. There is an immense clothing and jewelry market on the west side of the boulevard, that you can go through or around. Your route will be flanked by a number of hawkers selling mainly watches and sunglasses, though their

wares may change with the season. After passing under the *périphérique* (and through another big clothing market), turn left into rue des Rosiers. This long, straight street connects with the entrances to twelve individual markets aggregating more than 3,000 stalls. There are a dozen or more restaurants along the rue des Rosiers, some quite inviting, to which you may return later, exhausted and famished. Saturday and Sunday are the high traffic days in Clignancourt, while Monday is relatively quiet (though not all vendors are open).

We happen to like the Marché Dauphine for its visual appeal, the fact that it's well organized under a glass roof, and because it even has its own small café. Dauphine is open the same hours as the other markets, but also Friday from 8 am to noon. If you're seriously seeking something in a particular style or period, your visit will be more productive with a copy of *Tout Paris* or *Antique & Flea Markets of London & Paris* (see the bibliography) in hand. If you plan to make expensive purchases, you might consider using a certified expert in the field. To make this connection, the Office of Tourism can be helpful. You'll find it at 10, Impasse Simon, on the south side of rue des Rosiers just after the Marché Paul-Bert/Serpette.

A small *brocante* market, the Marché à la Ferraille, holds forth on the rue Jean-Henri Fabre, which parallels the *périphérique*. A determined visitor can still find bargains here.

BROCANTE FAIRS

It's impossible to find and describe all the markets of Paris, in part because some are temporary neighborhood flea markets set up on a Saturday morning and taken down by Sunday afternoon. We think of them as *brocante* fairs; the only reliable way to know when and where to find them is to watch for colorful banners and posters that announce them a week or ten days in advance. Some fairs are repeat visitors to the host site, but many of the vendors—mainly of flea market goods—are birds of passage. We've talked with a few who have told us where they might be a week or two in the future, but this hardly seems like reliable information. Take them for what they are—pleasant surprises that may yield an item that has long been on your search list and that suddenly, fortuitously, presents itself.

Saint-Pierre Fabric Market

LE MARCHÉ SAINT-PIERRE

Place Saint-Pierre at the corner of rue Livingstone, 18th arr.

🚇 *Barbès-Rochechouart*

Monday to Saturday 9 am to 6 pm

Le Marché Saint-Pierre is in an old wooden building that houses five floors of fabrics of every imaginable color, texture, weave, and print. Le Marché Reine across the street is a competitor, but the prices, the variety, and the quality at Saint-Pierre make it worth the trip.

To reach this unusual fabric market, take the métro to Barbès-Rochechouart, exit to the north, and go west along the boulevard Rochechouart. Turn right on rue Clignancourt, and take the first left on rue d'Orsel. A number of specialty stores on this street stock buttons, braid, and fabric trimmings of all kinds, as well as some specialty fabrics. Village d'Orsel also has ready-made sheets, pillowcases, and bedcovers at bargain prices, as well as quality handbags, luggage, and leather goods.

Moline, a large shop on the approach to place Saint-Pierre, has an impressive inventory of fabrics as well as all the hooks, buttons, fringes, bangles, and beads that decorators adore.

Each floor is devoted to fabrics for different purposes. On the ground floor are leftovers and bargains. The 1st floor (2nd in American parlance) is your destination if you want to take away something colorful and portable: among the alternatives are dishtowels and table settings, napkins, chair covers, sheets, pillowcases, and small cushions. Be aware that the dimensions are based on centimeters, not inches, and that the size and shape of most items will reflect European, not American, cultural norms.

Throughout the store, young salesmen in jeans and tee shirts carry the tools of their trade: a meter stick, a pair of scissors, a ballpoint pen, and a receipt book. They measure and rip off the length of material requested, and fill out a payment form, which is taken to the cashier before collecting one's purchases. Admonitions such as "*Nous ne donnons pas d'échatillons*" (We don't give samples) are painted on the overhead beams and on the stair risers. And it's impossible to miss the frequently stenciled warning, "Every sale is final."

Across the street (rue R. P. Picard) is Saint-Pierre Mercier, which sells every kind of hardware associated with every conceivable use of fabric.

19TH ARRONDISSEMENT • BUTTES-CHAUMONT

FOOD MARKETS

Crimée-Curial Open-Air Food Market • 250

Jean Jaurès Open-Air Food Market • 250

Joinville Open-Air Food Market • 251

Place des Fêtes Open-Air Food Market • 253

Porte Brunet Open-Air Food Market • 253

Porte d'Aubervilliers Open-Air Food Market • 254

Villette Open-Air Food Market • 254

Crimée-Curial Open-Air Food Market

LE MARCHÉ CRIMÉE-CURIAL
Intersection of the rue de Crimée and rue de Curial, 19th arr.
🚇 *Crimée*
Tuesday and Friday 8 am to 1 pm

Along with the big Franprix supermarket on the corner, a tiny market of half a dozen stands loyally serves its neighborhood. Neither is of serious interest to the traveler.

Jean Jaurès Open-Air Food Market

LE MARCHÉ JEAN-JAURÈS
North side of avenue Jean-Jaurès between rue de l'Ourcq and rue des Ardennes, 19th arr.
🚇 *Ourcq*
Tuesday, Thursday, and Sunday 8 am to 1 pm

An excellent small market serves this working-class part of Paris, with every kind of fresh meat, fish, cheese, and produce at reasonable prices. Vendors are little concerned with beautiful displays for shoppers or travelers, but the atmosphere is friendly and businesslike.

Joinville Open-Air Food Market

In the late 1800s, the gradual closure of numerous covered markets led to the creation of outdoor markets to accommodate merchants whose space had been eliminated. Joinville was one of those, established in 1873 and still going strong. Stalls fill the pavement between the old church of Saint-Jacques and Saint-Christophe on one side and modern apartment buildings on the other. Shouts of *"Allez! Allez!"* and *"La, la, la"* compete with each other as vendors encourage customers to buy their goods. Friendly repartee sets the tone as sellers goad each other

and joke with customers. A multicultural crowd shops here, predominantly Muslim and Chinese. Most customers pull shopping carts stuffed to the brim with the morning's purchases.

Plentiful vegetables and fruits can be found for sale individually or in three- and five-kilo bags. Prices are low and quality varies. As piles diminish, they're hurriedly replenished from crates stored in trucks parked along the periphery. Inexpensive *culottes* (women's underwear) and bins of household goods from soaps and sponges to batteries and drain catchers offer opportunities for impulse purchases. Point to an item, and the vendor will reach with a long pole and present it to you in a netted basket—a *marché* version of a butterfly net.

For a break from the noisy hubbub, step away from the southern edge of the market and enjoy views of the Canal de l'Ourcq, where tourist boats chug peacefully toward the Parc de la Villette.

Place des Fêtes Open-Air Food Market

LE MARCHÉ PLACE DES FÊTES

Place des Fêtes, 19th arr.

🚇 *Place des Fêtes*

Tuesday, Friday, and Sunday 8 am to 1 pm

This is one of the largest markets far from the center of Paris; the convenience of the métro makes a point in its favor, and most of the food stalls offer fresh meat, fish, and produce as good as one can find elsewhere. But even a children's playground in the center of this huge open square does not offset the depressing effect of anonymous apartment buildings and unappealing stores around the perimeter.

Porte Brunet Open-Air Food Market

LE MARCHÉ PORTE BRUNET

Avenue de la Porte Brunet, from boulevard Sérrurier to boulevard d'Indochine-boulevard d'Algérie, 19th arr.

🚇 *Danube*

Wednesday and Saturday 8 am to 1 pm

Coming up from the métro into the lovely little place de Rhin et Danube is like entering another world: quiet streets, small brick houses, low-profile apartment buildings, and grand old sycamore trees. This pleasant place also has a classic collection of neighborhood food shops.

Porte d'Aubervilliers Open-Air Food Market

LE MARCHÉ PORTE D'AUBERVILLIERS
Avenue de la Porte d'Aubervilliers, 19th arr.
🚇 *Porte de la Chapelle*
Wednesday and Saturday 8 am to 1 pm

This tiny market in a neighborhood of bleak brick apartments can vary from a single vegetable stand on a cold, rainy day to a dozen diverse stalls in good weather. The site on the northern edge of Paris is not pretty, but the people who live here want fresh food, and this is where they get it.

Villette Open-Air Food Market

LE MARCHÉ DE LA VILLETTE
Median plaza of boulevard de la Villette, from rue Burnouf to
rue Rébeval, 19th arr.
🚇 *Belleville*
Wednesday and Saturday 8 am to 1 pm

Essentially, this market is an extension of the Marché de Belleville, held Tuesday and Friday on the same median plaza, south of the Belleville métro station. Old sycamores make it more pleasant to shop than the treeless upper part of the neighboring Belleville market.

20TH ARRONDISSEMENT ✦ BELLEVILLE

FOOD MARKETS

Belgrand Open-Air Food Market ✦ 256

Davout Open-Air Food Market ✦ 256

Mortier Open-Air Food Market ✦ 257

Père-Lachaise Open-Air Food Market ✦ 257

Pyrénées Open-Air Food Market ✦ 258

Reunion Open-Air Food Market ✦ 258

Télégraphe Open-Air Food Market ✦ 259

MARKETPLACES

Book and Paper Market ✦ 261

Porte de Montreuil Flea Market ✦ 263

Belgrand Open-Air Food Market

LE MARCHÉ BELGRAND

North side of rue Belgrand from place Edith Piaf to rue de la Chine; both sides of rue de la Chine from rue Belgrand to avenue Gambetta, 20th arr.

🚇 *Porte de Bagnolet, Gambetta*

Wednesday 8 am to 1:30 pm; Saturday 8 am to 2 pm

The Belgrand market seems to go on forever, a vast wealth of foodstuff and clothing. It is remarkably diverse for a market so far from the center of Paris. But it is usually crowded, indicating that local residents find it fills their needs.

Davout Open-Air Food Market

LE MARCHÉ DAVOUT

East side of boulevard Davout from avenue de la Porte de Montreuil to place Marie de Mirabel, 20th arr.

🚇 *Porte de Montreuil*

Tuesday and Friday 8 am to 1:30 pm

There are many produce stands in this market, and some novelties such as an herbalist who sells soap from Provence, and a cheese merchant from the island of Mauritius. The color and aroma of the hams at Jambon à l'Ancienne appeal to us, as does the *poissonnier* Méchet, whose stand has a properly briny smell. He sells chunks of fish for soup at bargain prices.

Mortier Open-Air Food Market

LE MARCHÉ MORTIER
Boulevard Mortier, from avenue de la Porte de Ménilmontant to rue Maurice Bertaux, 20th arr.
🚇 *Saint-Fargeau, Porte de Bagnolet*
Wednesday 8 am to 1:30 pm; Sunday 8 am to 2 pm

A gently sloping street with old sycamores lining broad sidewalks gives this market an appearance strangely akin to a London suburb. It has the neighborly feel particular to many outlying areas of Paris. Monsieur Petit offers pristine goat cheeses, made at home from the milk of goats raised by him.

Père-Lachaise Open-Air Food Market

LE MARCHÉ PÈRE-LACHAISE
Boulevard de Ménilmontant from rue des Panoyaux to rue des Cendriers, 20th arr.
🚇 *Ménilmontant*
Tuesday and Friday 8 am to 1:30 pm

This small market offers quality produce and friendly vendors. When we visited, eggs were sold by weight in one-cent increments from the smallest to the largest.

Pyrénées Open-Air Food Market

LE MARCHÉ PYRÉNÉES
*Rue des Pyrénées between the rue de l'Ermitage and
the rue de Ménilmontant, 20th arr.*
🚇 *Pyrénées, Jourdain*
Thursday 8 am to 1:30 pm; Sunday 8 am to 2 pm

Display gets scant attention in this market. The ambience is friendly, the presentation direct. We were drawn to Senteurs de Provence at 282, rue des Pyrénées, selling lavender, honey, candles, fabric, santons, and other regional products.

Réunion Open-Air Food Market

LE MARCHÉ RÉUNION
Place de la Réunion, 20th arr.
🚇 *Alexandre Dumas*
Thursday 8 am to 1:30 pm; Sunday 8 am to 2 pm

One of the larger markets on the outskirts of Paris, place de la Réunion caters to younger shoppers who have less to spend but bring the same insistence on *qualité-prix*, or value for money. At Grandjean, stainless steel pans are filled with cooked dishes ready to go: *tripes à la mode de Caen, légumes à la Provençale, choucroute, sauté de porc à la Pékinoise,* freshly grilled sausages, and hot braised hams.

Télégraphe Open-Air Food Market

Water towers and a radio mast on the hilltop beside the cemetery signal this small neighborhood market in a distant part of Paris. There is the usual array of produce stands, cheese sellers, and fishmongers. Yannick Lebert's refrigerated butcher stand may give shoppers extra confidence in modern methods of maintaining freshness.

PARIS
PARIS 19eme
PARIS
PARIS 17eme
6eme
PARIS 5eme
4eme
PARIS 3eme

Book and Paper Market

LE MARCHÉ AUX VIEUX PAPIERS
Porte de Vincennes, avenue de Paris, from rue Faÿs to
place de la Prévoyance, just outside the 20th arr.
🚇 *Saint-Mandé-Tourelle*
Wednesday 9 am to 6 pm

This market is not, strictly speaking, in Paris, but it's definitely of Paris
—a fascinating place to stroll down France's memory lane. People come
here to look for a postcard mailed from their native village. Tens of
thousands of used cards are indexed geographically for France and its
overseas dependencies, or by subject matter, while foreign cards are filed
by country of origin.

The boxes of postcards are usually turned so that clients cannot
riffle through them but must ask for what they want. The dealer de-
termines whether it's available, and hands over a selection for review.
A few boxes are arranged by rubrics such as sports or leisure activities,
and turned so browsing clients can serve themselves. The price of a card
averages one or two euros, but rare items may cost twenty-five or more.

Beyond the postcard collections that make up the core of this market, used books constitute the major items for sale. In addition, there is
an amazing variety of small things made of paper: bar coasters (known
as *sous-bock*), matchboxes, small colored cards with religious homilies
(*chromos*), old letters, comic books, movie posters, paperback books,
magazines, matchbook-covers, 33 $^1/_3$ and 45 rpm record covers, and eso-
teric collectibles that are impossible to find elsewhere.

C'est la mèr' Michel
qui a perdu son chat,
Qui cri'. par la f'nêtre
à qui le lui rendra,
Et l' compèr' Lustucru
qui lui a répondu :
Allez, la mèr' Michel,
vot' chat n'est pas perdu.

Edité par DE RICQLÈS et Cie

A prominent paper collectible is trading cards. Most relate to U.S. sports teams, along with an impressive variety of other subjects such as rock music, classical music, history, film, and sports. Europeans avidly trade soccer and rugby cards, ninety percent of which are manufactured in and distributed from the United States.

A few of the stalls slip into flea market goods, such as CDs and DVDs, telephone cards, caps from champagne corks, brooches, key rings, foreign coins, and even old Barbie and G.I. Joe dolls. There are military medals, whole armies of miniature soldiers, and peculiar little ceramic figurines called *fèves*, some resembling the three magi. Traditionally, *fève* beans were baked into a cake served the Twelfth Night after Christmas. The person in whose slice the *fève* was found became king or queen for a day. Now these tiny objects have replaced the bean.

Porte de Montreuil Flea Market

LE MARCHÉ AUX PUCES DE MONTREUIL
*Avenue du Professeur André Lemierre at
place de la Porte de Montreuil, 20th arr.*
🚇 *Porte de Montreuil*
Saturday, Sunday, and Monday 7 am to 7:30 pm

There is a rough edge in this market that, while not threatening, is a bit off-putting. Montreuil is different from the Vanves flea market, and may be of less interest to the casual visitor. Nevertheless, it has a grittiness and diversity that makes it memorable for adventuresome shoppers.

From the subway exit, cross over the *périphérique* and enter a market so vast and crowded it's impossible to explore in an hour. Smooth-talking young African men with collapsible tables may be scattered around the place de Montreuil, tempting the crowd with a game of chance. The challenge is to guess which of three cards will show up in the left, right, and center positions. A lot of money changes hands here.

The jam in the aisles makes this market a tumultuous experience. You can buy new goods in their original shrink-wrapped cartons. A few stands offer the lamps, glassware, table settings, and household bric-a-brac (*brocante*) that are standard flea market fare, but the main focus of this market is hardware. There is a vast selection of items such as electric drills, sanding machines, wrench sets, and toolboxes, all offered at shockingly low prices. In addition, everything for the fully supplied kitchen is here, mostly new, as well as professional and household hardware.

There are mounds of clothing that buyers must paw through to find what they want: Shirts, underwear, and socks make up the bulk of it. You can find running shoes and leather shoes, hats and scarves, skirts and sweaters, down jackets and leather jackets, along with a proliferation of blouses and trousers too great to describe. You might come here to look for a wristwatch, a clock-radio, a professional sausage-slicer, a hair-dryer, electric wall switches, or replacement parts for cars. Perhaps you're shopping for soap, toothbrushes, or hand and body lotion. It's all here, and more, but remember, *caveat emptor*.

On Ascension Day and Toussaint, an event called a *grand déballage* (a big unpacking) brings in a flood of dealers, shoppers, and gawkers.

Eating Out in Paris

Years ago, the word restaurant in French described an establishment that met certain qualifications and expectations in the minds of clients, as in the minds of government officials who awarded licenses. It meant a white cloth on the table, an elaborate menu, and a highly professional serving staff. Nowadays it hardly conveys anything meaningful, other than that food is served.

The *brasserie* was born as a beer-hall in Alsace, the region where France and Germany share a border. It's less self-conscious about its cooking. *Brasserie* food is basic food, everything the French love from traditional *oeufs mayonnaise* to *steak au poivre*, *pommes frites*, and *crème caramel*. The most reliable meals in Paris are available at *brasseries*. Serving is continuous during the day, and they are open late at night, on weekends, and Mondays when most restaurants traditionally are closed.

We adore the food and ambience of the *brasserie*, and have a special fondness for big, bustling Bofinger in the 4th arrondissement. A junior edition of Bofinger can be found across the street. The *brasserie* at the Hôtel Lutétia in the 6th arrondissement is as close to a deluxe establishment as one can find. Brasserie Lipp, on boulevard Saint-Germain in the 6th arrondissement since 1880, has been and still is the place to get a glimpse of France's political, artistic, and intellectual glitterati.

A *bistro* is a small, family-style restaurant, often with a lively sense of its place in the firmament. Most offer traditional fare, though there is a movement toward experimental cooking in some, such as Les

Bistronomes in the 1st, Christophe in the 5th, Le Bistrot Paul Bert in the 11th, and Le Baratin in the 20th arrondissement. A classic and favorite of ours is Le Bistrot d'Henri in the 6th.

The straightforward but essential *café* is a basic feature of alimentary and social life outside the home. There is one in nearly every block in Paris, often with tables on the sidewalk in the sun. Coffee, beer, and wine are the mainstays of the *café*, but simple food is also available, served quickly from a limited but hearty menu. Big, bustling places like the Deux Magots and the Flore on boulevard Saint-Germain are true *cafés*, but they are the racehorses of the breed, not the workhorses.

Not to be overlooked is the humble *bar*. Sometimes it will be the only thing in sight for a coffee and a croissant on a cold day, or to make a bathroom stop (don't expect to use the *toilettes* unless you buy a coffee). It may look dark and dingy, but *le bar* is a reservoir of warmth and goodwill for the visitor who may need it in a pinch.

Everywhere, *le menu* means the meal of the day, while *la carte* is the list of food and drink. Establishments of all kinds generally stop serving lunch by three o'clock, some earlier. And don't expect to arrive for dinner before seven. If you do, you may see the kitchen and wait staff clustered around a back table, enjoying a jovial meal together before work begins.

We've provided a list of reasonably priced restaurants, brasseries, bistros, and wine bars organized by arrondissement. We've frequented many of them, and our friends many others, but don't take our word for it; experience will guide you to your own wonderful discoveries.

Restaurants

Finding a restaurant in Paris is easy, but finding one that fits the mood of the moment, where honest food is served, where one is treated with courtesy and leaves with a sense of gratitude, is difficult. Not every restaurant in this list is guaranteed to satisfy these criteria—one might not leave Brasserie Lipp with a sense of gratitude—but something about each of them might fit the mood of the moment. *Bonne chance, et bon appétit!*

1ST ARRONDISSEMENT

LES CARTES POSTALES

7, rue Gomboust, 01 42 61 02 93, 🚇 Pyramides. Tuesday to Sunday to 10:30 pm; closed Saturday lunch, Sunday, and Monday dinner. A talented Japanese chef serves innovative dishes in a charming venue.

PAUL

15, place Dauphine/35, quai des Orfevres, 01 43 54 21 48, 🚇 Cité. Tuesday to Sunday to 10:30 pm; closed Monday. You can dine outdoors on the Seine side or on the lovely (and quiet) place Dauphine side. Inside are dark wood, banquettes, and classic dishes at reasonable prices. Service is friendly and impeccable.

AU PIED DE COCHON

6, rue Coquillière, 01 40 13 77 00, 🚇 les Halles. Daily, 24 hours. This venerable establishment once drew its victuals from the huge Les Halles market. Famous for everything porcine, especially trotters (they also serve shellfish), it has a buzz and savoir-faire that make it worth a visit.

LE RESTAURANT DU PALAIS ROYAL

110, galerie de Valois—Jardin du Palais Royal, 01 40 20 00 27, 🚇 Palais Royal-Musée du Louvre. Daily to 10:30 pm; closed Saturday (October to April) and Sunday (summer). This is a wonderful location in the heart of the heart of Paris, with a traditional setting and pure comfort food.

ROUGE SAINT-HONORÉ

34, place du Marché St-Honoré, 01 42 61 16 09, 🚇 Pyramides, Tuileries. Reportedly open every day for lunch and dinner, an unassuming and inexpensive café in a lovely setting.

LE SOUFFLÉ

36, rue du Mont-Thabor, 01 42 60 27 19, 🚇 Tuileries, Concorde. Monday to Saturday to 10 pm. A small, friendly restaurant specializing in soufflés, but with other offerings as well. Food and service excellent, slightly formal but not pretentious.

WILLI'S WINE BAR

13, rue des Petits-Champs, 01 42 61 05 09, 🚇 Bourse, Palais Royal–Musée du Louvre. Monday to Saturday to 11 pm; closed Sunday. Willi's has gotten high marks over the years from all the reputable French and American reviewers, and deserves them.

2ND ARRONDISSEMENT

CHEZ GEORGES

1, rue du Mail, 01 42 60 07 11, 🚇 Bourse, Sentier. Monday to Saturday to 9:45 pm; closed Sunday. This classic bistro serves dishes that can vary from day to day. When they're good, they approach perfection, and when they're not, they are less than reliable.

L'ESCARGOT MONTORGUEIL

38, rue Montorgueil, 01 42 36 83 51, 🚇 Les Halles. Monday to Saturday to 11 pm; closed all day Sunday and Monday lunch. This lovely small bistro has descended from an earlier era; standard fare, but perfect ambience.

LE GRAND COLBERT

2, rue Vivienne, 01 42 86 87 88, 🚇 Bourse. Daily noon to 1 am. Decorated in the belle époque style; classic dishes served with panache.

3ᴿᴰ ARRONDISSEMENT

AU BASCOU

38, rue Réaumur, 01 42 72 69 25, 🚇 Arts et Métiers. Monday to Friday to 10:30 pm; closed Saturday and Sunday. Come here for Basque cooking at its best in a friendly and informal environment.

ROBERT ET LOUISE

64, rue Vieille-du-Temple, 01 42 78 55 89, 🚇 Rambuteau. Daily to 10:30 pm. Steak grilled on an open fire, communal tables, great neighborhood charm—this place will never disappoint.

4ᵀᴴ ARRONDISSEMENT

LA BARACANE

38, rue des Tournelles, 01 42 71 43 33, 🚇 Bastille. Monday to Friday to midnight; closed Saturday and Sunday. A great bistro featuring the cooking of the southwest; service a bit slow but atmosphere engaging.

BENÔIT

20, rue Saint-Martin, 01 42 72 25 76, 🚇 Châtelet, Hôtel de Ville. Monday to Saturday to 10 pm; closed Saturday lunch and Sunday. A classic in all respects, from the decor to the menu. Its Michelin star is well deserved.

BOFINGER

5 and 7, rue de la Bastille, 01 42 72 87 82, 🚇 Bastille. Daily to 1 am. The oldest brasserie in Paris (1864), with turn-of-the-century decor and a pleasing menu.

AU BOUGNAT

26, rue Chanoinesse, 01 43 54 50 74, 🚇 Cité, Hôtel de Ville. Daily 10 am to 10 pm. A small, friendly neighborhood restaurant and wine bar. The food is simple, but good and not expensive. Service outstanding.

MA BOURGOGNE

19, place des Vosges, 01 42 78 44 64, 🚇 Bastille. Daily 8 am to 1:30 am. In a welcoming corner location, this is the place for a coffee and croissant, a salad, or a drink; the food menu is limited.

LE DÔME BASTILLE

2, rue de la Bastille, 01 48 04 88 44, 🚇 Bastille. Daily to 11 pm. You will find here the same good management and fine seafood that one finds at Le Dôme and its neighboring bistro in the 14th arrondissement.

MON VIEIL AMI

69, rue Saint Louis en l'Île, 01 40 46 01 35, 🚇 Pont Marie. Wednesday to Sunday for lunch and dinner. Inventive reinterpretations of French classics, with an emphasis on vegetables.

PETIT BOFINGER

6, rue de la Bastille, 01 42 72 05 23, 🚇 Bastille. Daily to 1 am. A fabulous fallback when the main restaurant across the street is full, and food that may be just as good at a more attractive price.

5ᵀᴴ ARRONDISSEMENT

LE BAR À HUITRES

33, rue Saint-Jacques, 01 44 07 27 37, 🚇 Cluny-La Sorbonne. Daily noon to midnight. Reliable seafood, especially fresh, succulent oysters.

LE BISTRO CÔTÉ MER

16, boulevard Saint-Germain, 01 43 54 59 10, 🚇 Maubert-Mutualité. Monday to Saturday to 11 pm; closed Saturday lunch and Sunday. Crisp, congenial service; the food will not disappoint.

BRASSERIE BALZAR

49, rue des Écoles, 01 43 54 13 67, 🚇 Cluny-la Sorbonne, Odéon. Daily to midnight. This beloved brasserie almost disappeared when new owners took over. It survives with a revised menu, but the same art deco interior, attentive service, and reliable dishes classically prepared.

CHANTAIRELLE

17, rue Laplace, 01 46 33 18 59, 🚇 Maubert-Mutualité. Monday to Saturday to 10:30 pm; closed Saturday lunch and Sunday. You'll find superb country specialties of the Auvergne in this modern bistro.

ITINÉRAIRES

5, rue de Pontoise, 01 46 33 60 11, 🚇 Maubert-Mutualité. Monday to Friday noon to 2 pm and 7 to 10:30 pm. One of the friendliest places where we have dined in a long time. Attentive staff, inventive dishes. Perhaps a bit pricey, but worth the expense.

MOISSONNIER

28, rue des Fossés-Saint-Bernard, 01 43 29 87 65, 🚇 Cardinal Lemoine. Tuesday to Saturday to 10 pm; closed Sunday and Monday. Food is in the Lyonnais bistro tradition—lots of it and quite good.

AU MOULIN À VENT

20, rue des Fossés Saint-Bernard, 01 43 54 99 37, 🚇 Cardinal Lemoine. Tuesday to Saturday to 11 pm; closed Saturday lunch, all day Sunday and Monday. This traditional bistro has hardly changed since World War II, though meat specialties have kept pace with demand.

LE PRÉ VERRE

8, rue Thénard, 01 43 54 59 47, 🚇 Maubert-Mutualité. Tuesday to Saturday for lunch and dinner. We choose the fixed-price menu for an affordable three-course meal based on seasonal ingredients and bold flavor combinations.

LE REMINET

3, rue des Grands-Degrés, 01 44 07 04 24, 🚇 Maubert-Mutualité. Closed Tuesday and Wednesday. A long, narrow room is made romantic with candles, mirrors, and chandeliers. An appealing menu, though tables are a bit close.

LA RÔTISSERIE DU BEAUJOLAIS

19, quai de la Tournelle, 01 43 54 17 47, 🚇 Maubert-Mutualité. Tuesday to Sunday to 10:15 pm; closed Monday. The same owner as the fabled Tour d'Argent across the way; this Lyonnais-style bistro is lively and stocks all ten crus of Beaujolais.

ALLARD

1, rue de l'Éperon, 01 43 26 48 23, 🚇 Saint-Michel, Odéon. Monday to Saturday to 11 pm; closed Sunday. We've been up and down about this place. It may depend on who is in the kitchen. Sometimes it's incredibly good, and sometimes just okay. They say they're open every day, but that has yet to be proven.

LA BASTIDE ODÉON

7, rue Corneille, 01 43 26 03 65, 🚇 Odéon, Luxembourg. Tuesday to Saturday to 10:30 pm; closed Sunday and Monday. Proud of their nouvelle cuisine menu and their Provençale tilt, they are good, but at a price.

LE BISTROT D'HENRI

16, rue Princesse, 01 46 33 51 12, 🚇 Mabillon. Daily to 11:30 pm. Cigarette smoke used to drive us crazy, but when the rules changed qualité-prix brought us back. Tables from recycled sewing machines, moleskin banquettes, and an open kitchen conspire to create hustle and charm.

BOUILLON RACINE

3, rue Racine, 01 44 32 15 60, 🚇 Odéon, Cluny-la Sorbonne. Daily noon to midnight. Perhaps the best Belgian restaurant in Paris, its selection of native beers accompanies classic dishes of France's northern neighbor. High-quality art deco interior, a quiet environment, and a very pleasant bar.

LES BOUQUINISTES

53, quai des Grands-Augustins, 01 43 25 45 94, 🚇 Saint-Michel. Monday to Saturday to 11 pm; closed Saturday lunch and Sunday. Views of the

Quai, and a sense of high energy; the food has never disappointed us, though it's a bit pricey.

BRASSERIE LIPP

151, boulevard Saint-Germain, 01 45 48 53 91, 🚇 Saint-Germain-des-Prés. Daily noon to 1 am. The food may be mundane and the service somewhat casual, but this is where France's intellectual and political classes act like ordinary mortals with appetites. Try to be seated on the ground floor, not upstairs with the hoi-polloi.

BREAD & ROSES

7, rue de Fleurus, 01 42 22 06 06, 🚇 Rennes. (Another location at 25, rue Boissy d'Anglas, 8th arrondissement, 01 47 42 40 40, Métro: Madeleine.) 8 am to 8 pm Monday to Saturday. Organic breads and high-quality ingredients make every snack or meal here delicious and nutritious. Emphasis is on simple preparations that let the fresh ingredients speak for themselves.

LE CHERCHE-MIDI

22, rue du Cherche-Midi, 01 45 48 27 44, 🚇 Sèvres-Babylone. Daily noon to 11:45 pm. We were nearly buried by a busload of Japanese tourists, but we all were served promptly and ate well. A good port in a storm.

LES ÉDITEURS

4, carrefour de l'Odéon, 01 43 26 67 76, 🚇 Odéon. Continuous service from 8 am to 2 am. One goes here more to be seen than to find great food on the table, but the location is prime and standard dishes are reliably presented.

L'ÉPI DUPIN

11, rue Dupin, 01 42 22 64 56, 🚇 Sèvres-Babylone. Monday dinner to Friday at 11 pm; closed all day Saturday, Sunday, and Monday lunch. Interesting dishes at acceptable prices, but getting a reservation has been difficult even though they turn tables rapidly.

FISH LA BOISSONNERIE, RESTAURANT MÉDITERRANÉEN

69, rue de Seine, 01 43 54 34 69, 🚇 Mabillon. Closed Monday. We got to know co-owner Juan Sanchez when he opened La Dernière Goute, a small wine shop around the corner. Naturally we became clients when he opened Fish. The fresh catch and the pasta always please.

ROGER LA GRENOUILLE

26-28, rue des Grands-Augustins, 01 56 24 24 44, 🚇 Odéon. Tuesday to Saturday to 11 pm; closed all day Sunday and Monday lunch. We didn't actually have a meal here, but it looked so charming from the street that we thought we would go back sometime. A long, narrow dining room is accessed from an adjacent courtyard. The same owners as Allard, which could be a good recommendation.

LA RÔTISSERIE D'EN FACE

2, rue Christine, 01 43 26 40 98, 🚇 Odéon. Monday to Friday to 11:30 pm, closed Saturday lunch and all day Sunday. The second kitchen of Jacques Cagna, whose main establishment is a few steps away, offers an appealing menu, a lovely dining room, and attentive service.

7TH ARRONDISSEMENT

LE BAMBOCHE

15, rue de Babylone, 01 45 49 14 40, 🚇 Sèvres-Babylone. Daily to 10 pm; closed Sunday lunch. For their elegant portions, interesting choices, and romantic dining room, we keep going back.

AU BON ACCUEIL

14, rue de Monttessuy, 01 47 05 46 11, 🚇 Alma-Marceau. Monday to Friday to 10 pm; closed Saturday lunch and Sunday. Established, reliable, with elements of tradition and modernity, it's always busy, so book ahead. We try to time our exit for the top of the hour to enjoy the Eiffel Tower sparkling nearby.

LA LAITERIE SAINTE-CLOTILDE

64, rue de Bellechasse, 01 45 51 74 61, 🚇 Solférino. Monday to Saturday for lunch and dinner. Reasonable prices and a simple chalkboard menu based on market-fresh ingredients make this a neighborhood gem. It is popular with a hip crowd, so reservations are a must.

LES MINISTÈRES

30, rue du Bac, 01 42 61 22 37, 🚇 Rue du Bac. Daily to 10 pm. Good location near the Seine. Since 1919, this has been a classic spot with reasonable prices, every dish presented *comme il faut.*

OUDINO

17, rue Oudinot, 01 45 66 05 09, 🚇 Vaneau. Monday to Saturday for lunch and dinner. The lamb shoulder that has been cooked for seven hours to tender perfection is so heavenly that we have a hard time ordering anything else.

8ᵀᴴ ARRONDISSEMENT
L´ÉCLUSE

15, place de la Madeleine, 01 42 65 34 69, 🚇 Madeleine. Daily to 1 am. This wine bar specializing in Bordeaux, one of a chain of five around the city, offers a limited bistro menu. Also located at:

34, place du Marché Saint-Honoré, 1st arrondissement

15, quai des Grands-Augustins, 6th arrondissement

64, rue François 1er, 8th arrondissement

1, rue d'Armaillé, 17th arrondissement

TANTE LOUISE

41, rue Boissy-d'Anglas, 01 42 65 06 85, 🚇 Madeleine, Concorde. Monday to Friday to 10:30 pm; closed Saturday and Sunday. A Christmas Eve dinner here (le Réveillon) engraved itself on our hearts forever. Featuring a Burgundian menu, a fine wine list, and attentive service.

9ᵀᴴ ARRONDISSEMENT
ROSE BAKERY

46, rue des Martyrs, 01 42 82 12 80, 🚇 Pigalle, Saint-Georges. Tuesday to Saturday 9 am to 7 pm; Sunday 10 am to 6 pm; closed Monday. This tiny takeout lunch place has half a dozen small steel-topped tables, a variety of salads, and a few hot dishes, some with a British twist. Bargain prices for hearty organic food and a pleasant *vin de table* bring crowds at noon. Also at 30, rue Debelleyme, 3rd arrondissement, 🚇 Filles du Calvaire.

10ᵀᴴ ARRONDISSEMENT
LA GRILLE

80, rue du Faubourg-Poissonnière, 01 47 70 89 73, 🚇 Barbès-Rochechouart,

Poissonnière. Monday to Friday to 9:30 pm; closed Saturday and Sunday. An old-fashioned bistro of a type that may be going out of style.

11ᵀᴴ ARRONDISSEMENT

CHARDENOUX

1, rue Jules Vallès, 01 43 71 49 52, 🚇 Charonne. Daily to 11 pm. Come here for wonderful turn-of-the-century décor, a fabulous wine list, and absolutely reliable dishes.

JACQUES MÉLAC

42, rue Léon Frot, 01 40 09 93 37, 🚇 Charonne. Tuesday to Saturday to 10:30 pm; closed Sunday and Monday. This is simple home cooking, with a wine list full of enchanting discoveries.

AU VIEUX CHÊNE

2, rue du Dahomey, 01 43 71 67 68, 🚇 Faidherbe-Chaligny. Daily 8 pm to 11:30 pm. Excellent and imaginative bistro cooking at prices that are truly reasonable. Interesting selection of wines.

12ᵀᴴ ARRONDISSEMENT

LE BARON ROUGE

1, rue Théophile-Roussel, 01 43 43 14 32, 🚇 Ledru-Rollin. Daily 10 am to 2 pm, 5 pm to 10 pm; Friday and Saturday 10 am to 10 pm; Sunday 10 am to 4 pm; closed Monday. This popular and classic little wine bar behind the Beauvau covered market is a hoot, with oysters, bread and butter, and a brass band on weekends.

A LA BICHE AU BOIS

45, avenue Ledru-Rollin, 01 43 43 34 38, 🚇 Gare de Lyon. Monday to

Friday to 11 pm; closed Saturday, Sunday, and Monday lunch. There's an inclination toward the pretentious with a specialty of wild game, but our meal was superb. It's popular, so reserve.

L'ÉBAUCHOIR

43-45, rue de Citeaux, 01 23 42 49 31, 🚇 Faidherbe-Chaligny, Reuilly-Diderot. Monday to Saturday to 11 pm; closed Sunday and Monday lunch. Well-prepared food in an unadorned environment; simple, noisy, fast, and fun.

A LA FRÉGATE

30, avenue Ledru-Rollin, 01 43 43 90 32, 🚇 Gare de Lyon. Monday to Friday to 10 pm; closed Saturday and Sunday. Somewhat dark, but honest food in a pleasant ambience. Seafood recommended.

LA GAZZETTA

29, rue de Cotte, 01 43 47 47 05, 🚇 Ledru-Rollin. Tuesday to Saturday noon to 2:30 pm and 1 pm to 11 pm. A talented Swedish chef turns out inspired dishes at this restaurant which borders Marché d'Aligre. Best option is dinner, when a daring five-course menu is sure to delight the taste buds.

L'OULETTE

15, place Lachambaudie, 01 40 02 02 12, 🚇 Dugommier. Monday to Friday to 10:15 pm; closed Saturday and Sunday. Pretty little place in a hidden corner of Bercy; the cooking is inventive and satisfying.

LE QUINCY

28, avenue Ledru-Rollin, 01 46 28 46 76, 🚇 Gare de Lyon. Tuesday to Friday to 10:15 pm; closed Saturday, Sunday, and Monday. Traditional menu, somewhat expensive, but the food and ambience will not disappoint.

SARDEGNA A TAVOLA

1, rue de Cotte, 01 44 75 03 28, 🚇 Ledru-Rollin. Tuesday to Saturday for lunch; Monday to Saturday for dinner. A stone's throw from Marché d'Aligre and the Beauvau covered market, this restaurant turns out hearty, full-flavored Mediterranean dishes in a convivial atmosphere.

LE SQUARE TROUSSEAU

1, rue Antoine Vollon, 01 43 43 06 00, 🚇 Ledru-Rollin. Daily noon to midnight. Traditional bistro fare in an agreeable setting; often packed, so reserve.

LE TRAIN BLEU, GARE DE LYON

20, boulevard Diderot, 01 43 43 09 06, 🚇 Gare de Lyon. Daily to 10:45 pm. Above the waiting room you'll find yourself in a magnificent space under a gloriously painted ceiling. Classic brasserie food is somewhat expensive and not great, but reliable.

AU TROU GASCON

40, rue Taine, 01 43 44 34 26, 🚇 Daumesnil. Monday to Friday to 10 pm; closed Saturday and Sunday. The cooking of the southwest is at its best here. The wine list is replete with the pick of Bordeaux, and great Armagnac. We love all of it.

LES ZYGOMATES

7, rue de Capri, 01 40 19 93 04, 🚇 Daumesnil, Michel Bizot. Tuesday to Saturday to 10:15 pm; closed Sunday and Monday. A former butcher shop, noisy and crowded, but attractive prices may explain why it's hard to get a table.

13TH ARRONDISSEMENT

AU PETIT MARGUERY

9, boulevard de Port Royal, 01 43 31 58 59, 🚇 Gobelins. Tuesday to Saturday to 10:15 pm; closed Sunday and Monday. Generous portions and rapid service make this a good stop. Consider the hare.

14TH ARRONDISSEMENT

LE BAR À HUITRES

112, boulevard du Montparnasse, 01 43 20 71 01, 🚇 Vavin. Open continuously from noon to 12:30 am. This is a sister ship to the restaurant of the same name in the 5th arrondissement, and has all the same qualities and values.

LE BISTROT DU DÔME

1, rue Delambre, 01 43 35 42 00, 🚇 Vavin. Daily to 11 pm. Offshoot of Le Dôme, perhaps less impressive in décor but not as dear. For fish and shellfish, look no further.

LE DÔME

108, boulevard du Montparnasse, 01 43 35 25 81, 🚇 Vavin. Daily to midnight. If you crave seafood properly prepared, this is the place for it, in a beautiful belle époque brasserie.

PARNASSE 138

138, boulevard du Montparnasse, 01 43 20 47 87, 🚇 Vavin, Port-Royale. Daily to 11:15 pm. Not stylish, but welcoming and serious about their standard dishes.

15TH ARRONDISSEMENT

AFARIA

15, rue Desnouettes, 01 48 56 15 36, 🚇 Convention. Tuesday to Saturday for lunch and dinner. A short walk from Marché Convention, this pleasant restaurant serves Basque-inspired tapas and full meals. The menu is organized by themes that are confusing and mostly meaningless, but the food is outstanding.

LA CASSE NOIX

56, rue de la Fédération, 01 45 66 09 01, 🚇 Bir-Hakeim. Monday to Friday. A young chef/owner, trained in some of the city's toniest eating establishments, takes his talents to this casual, affordable bistro. A relative newcomer to the scene, it's getting a lot of buzz.

L'OSTRÉADE

11, boulevard de Vaugirard, 01 43 21 87 41, 🚇 Montparnasse-Bienvenue. Daily to 11:15 pm; closed Saturday and Sunday. This is a haven for the seafood lover; well-prepared dishes at attractive prices.

16TH ARRONDISSEMENT

LES CAVES ANGEVINES

Chez Clarisse, 2, place Léon Deubel, 01 42 88 88 93, 🚇 Porte de Saint-Cloud. Monday to Friday, 9 am to 4 pm; Thursday and Friday, 7 pm to midnight; closed Saturday and Sunday. A neighborhood wine bar recommended by friends, it has gained good reviews both by the clientele and by the food and drink press.

AU CLOCHER DU VILLAGE

8 bis, rue Verderet, 01 42 88 06 38, 🚇 Mirabeau, Église-d'Auteuil. Tuesday to Sunday noon to 10:30 pm. A cozy neighborhood bistro that we discovered when living in Paris in the 1960s. The decor has changed, but the food remains correct and reliable.

MAISON PRUNIER

16, avenue Victor-Hugo, 01 44 17 35 85, 🚇 Étoile, Kléber. Daily to 1 am; closed Sunday. The dining room evokes what fine dining used to be in art deco Paris. Fish dishes are their strong suit.

17TH ARRONDISSEMENT

LE BALLON DES TERNES

103, avenue des Ternes, 01 45 74 17 98, 🚇 Porte Maillot. Daily to midnight. A big, busy brasserie in the classic style; the food is always reliable.

19TH ARRONDISSEMENT

LA CAVE GOURMANDE

10, rue du Général-Brunet, 01 40 40 03 30, 🚇 Botzaris. Tuesday to Saturday to 11 pm; closed Sunday and Monday. A talented young chef and a clean, well-lighted bistro work well together.

20TH ARRONDISSEMENT

LES ALLOBROGES

71, rue des Grands-Champs, 01 43 73 40 00, 🚇 Maraîchers. Tuesday to Saturday to 10 pm; closed Sunday dinner and Monday. Far from central Paris, but the décor is pleasing, the menu intriguing, and the presentation appealing.

Helpful Books, Blogs, and Websites

Little is written about the markets of Paris. Most of the material in this book we observed directly. Occasionally, Le Figaro (Paris) or The Times (London) will publish something on markets. However, this short list may help readers pursue a particular interest in more depth.

Armstrong, Jack, and Delores Wilson, *Boulangerie: Pocket Guide to Paris's Famous Bakeries* (Ten Speed Press, 2004).

Ballard, Ginette (ed.), *Secrets of Paris: A Guidebook for the Discerning Traveler* (Thomasson-Grant, 1994).

Bernstein, Michael A., *The Paris Guide*, Fourth Edition (Michael A. Bernstein, 32 Country Lane, Napa Valley, CA 94558, April 2004).

Cahill, Jamie, *The Pâtisseries of Paris* (The Little Bookroom, 2008).

Clemente, Maribeth, *The Riches of Paris: A Shopping and Touring Guide* (St. Martin's Griffin, 2007).

Downie, David, *Paris, Paris: Journey into the City of Light* (Broadway Books, 2011).

Drake, Alicia, *A Shopper's Guide to Paris Fashion* (Metro, 2000).

Dusoulier, Clotilde, *Clotilde's Edible Adventures in Paris* (Broadway Books, 2008).

Fierro, Alfred, *Historical Dictionary of Paris* (Scarecrow Press, 1998).

Gershman, Suzy, *Suzy Gershman's Born to Shop Paris* (Frommer's, 2009).

Gopnik, Adam, *Paris to the Moon* (Random House, 2001).

Hamburger, Robert and Barbara, *Bistros of Paris* (Ecco Press, 2001).

Jégu, Pierrick, *The Best Wine Bars and Shops of Paris* (The Little Bookroom, 2008).

Kaplan, Rachel, *Little-Known Museums In and Around Paris* (Harry N. Abrams, Inc., 1996).

Lebovitz, David, *The Sweet Life in Paris* (Broadway Books, 2011).

Lobrano, Alexander, *Hungry for Paris* (Random House, 2008).

Lown, Patricia Twohill and David, *All Paris* (The Palancar Co., Ltd., 2001).

Meyer, Nicolle Aimee, and Amanda Pilar Smith, *Paris in a Basket: Markets—the Food and the People* (Könemann, 2000).

Paris, Mode d'Emploi/User's Guide (Office de Tourism de Paris, 127, avenue des Champs-Elysées, 75008 Paris, n.d.).

Pudlowski, Gilles, *Pudlo Paris, 2007-2008* (The Little Bookroom, 2007).

Steinberger, Michael, *Au Revoir to All That: Food, Wine, and the End of France* (Bloomsbury USA, 2010).

Thomas, Rupert, and Eglé Salvy, *Antique and Flea Markets of London and Paris* (Thames and Hudson, 1999).

Thomazeau, François, and Sylvain Ageorges, *Authentic Bistros of Paris* (The Little Bookroom, 2005).

Webb, Michael, *Through the Windows of Paris: Fifty Unique Shops* (Princeton Architectural Press, 1999).

Wells, Patricia, *The Food Lover's Guide to Paris*, Fourth Edition (Workman Publishing Co., 1999).

Williams, Ellen, *The Historic Restaurants of Paris: A Guide to Century-Old Cafés, Bistros, and Gourmet Food Shops* (The Little Bookroom, 2001).

Young, Daniel, *Paris Café Cookbook* (William Morrow, 1998).

Zagat *Paris Restaurants* (Zagat Survey, 2010).

Zola, Émile, *The Belly of Paris*, translated by Brian Nelson (Oxford University Press, 2007).

SOME WEBSITES AND BLOGS WE LIKE

Alexander Lobrano • www.alexanderlobrano.com

Béatrice Peltre • www.latartinegourmande.com

Betty Rosbottom • www.bettyrosbottom.com/paris

Clotilde Dusoulier • www.chocolateandzucchini.com

David Lebovitz • www.davidlebovitz.com/paris

Dorie Greenspan • www.doriegreenspan.com/paris

Paris by Mouth • www.parisbymouth.com

The Paris Kitchen • www.thepariskitchen.com

Mairie de Paris • www.paris.fr

For detailed information on brocante fairs in French, go to
Paris Loisirs, Marchés, Programme des brocantes et vide-greniers.

Open on Sunday

1ST ARRONDISSEMENT

Saint-Eustache Les Halles Open-Air Food Market

Underground Shopping Centers

2ND ARRONDISSEMENT

Booksellers on the Seine

Covered Passages (Galerie Colbert-Galerie Vivienne,
Passage du Grand Cerf)

3RD ARRONDISSEMENT

Enfants Rouges Covered Food Market

4TH ARRONDISSEMENT

Booksellers on the Seine

The Flower and Bird Markets

Saint-Paul Antiques Village

5TH ARRONDISSEMENT

Place Monge Open-Air Food Market

Booksellers on the Seine

6TH ARRONDISSEMENT

Raspail Organic Open-Air Food Market

Saint-Germain Covered Food Market

Saint-Germain Art and Antiques Galleries

7TH ARRONDISSEMENT

Swiss Village Antiques

8TH ARRONDISSEMENT

Postage Stamp and Telephone Card Markets

9TH ARRONDISSEMENT

Covered Passages (Passage Jouffroy-Verdeau)

10TH ARRONDISSEMENT

Saint-Quentin Covered Food Market

Alibert Open-Air Food Market

Saint-Martin Covered Food Market

11TH ARRONDISSEMENT

Bastille Open-Air Food Market (also known as Richard Lenoir)

12TH ARRONDISSEMENT

Beauvau Covered Food Market

Bercy Open-Air Food Market

Poniatowski Open-Air Food Market

13TH ARRONDISSEMENT

Auguste-Blanqui Open-Air Food Market

Jeanne d'Arc Open-Air Food Market

Maison-Blanche Open-Air Food Market

14TH ARRONDISSEMENT

Villemain Open-Air Food Market

Edgar Quinet Arts and Crafts Market

Porte de Vanves Flea Market

15TH ARRONDISSEMENT

Grenelle Open-Air Food Market

Convention Open-Air Food Market

Antiquarian and Used Book Market

16TH ARRONDISSEMENT

Passy Covered Food Market

Point du Jour Open-Air Food Market

17TH ARRONDISSEMENT

Batignolles Covered Food Market

Ternes Covered Food Market

Place des Ternes Flower Market

18TH ARRONDISSEMENT

La Chapelle Covered Food Market

Ney Open-Air Food Market

Ordener Open-Air Food Market

Clignancourt Flea Market

19TH ARRONDISSEMENT

Joinville Open-Air Food Market

20TH ARRONDISSEMENT

Porte de Montreuil Flea Market

RESTAURANT INDEX

A

Afaria • 282
Allard • 273
Allobroges, Les • 284

B

Ballon des Ternes, Le • 283
Bamboche, Le • 276
Bar à Huitres, Le • 271, 281
Baracane, La • 269
Baron Rouge, Le • 278
Bascou, Au • 269
Bastide Odéon, La • 273
Benôit • 270
Biche au Bois, A la • 279

Bistro Côté Mer, Le • 271
Bistrot d'Henri, Le • 273
Bistrot du Dôme, Le • 281
Bofinger • 270
Bon Accueil, Au • 276
Bougnat, Au • 270
Bouillon Racine • 273
Bouquinistes, Les • 273
Brasserie Balzar • 271
Brasserie Lipp • 274
Bread & Roses • 274

C

Cartes Postales, Les • 267
Casse Noix, La • 282

Cave Gourmande, La • 283
Caves Angevines, Les • 282
Chantairelle • 271
Chardenoux • 278
Cherche-Midi, Le • 274
Chez Georges • 268
Clocher du Village, Au • 283

D
Dôme, Le • 281
Dôme Bastille, Le • 270

E
Ébauchoir, L' • 279
Écluse, L' • 277
Éditeurs, Les • 274
Épi Dupin, L' • 275
Escargot Montorgueil, L' • 269

F
Fish la Boissonnerie • 275
Frégate, A la • 279

G
Gazzetta, La • 279
Grand Colbert, Le • 269
Grille, La • 278

I
Itinéraires • 271

J
Jacques Mélac • 278

L
Laiterie Sainte-Clotilde, La • 276

M
Ma Bourgogne • 270
Maison Prunier • 283
Ministères, Les • 276
Moissonnier • 272
Mon Vieil Ami • 270
Moulin à Vent, Au • 272

O
Ostréade, L' • 282
Oudino • 276
Oulette, L' • 279

P
Parnasse 138 • 282
Paul • 267
Petit Bofinger • 271
Petit Marguery, Au • 281
Pied de Cochon, Au • 267
Pré Verre, Le • 272

Q
Quincy, Le • 280

R
Reminet, Le • 272
Restaurant du Palais Royal, Le • 268
Robert et Louise • 269
Roger La Grenouille • 275
Rose Bakery • 277
Rôtisserie d'en Face, La • 275
Rôtisserie du Beaujolais, La • 272
Rouge Saint-Honoré • 268

S
Sardegna a Tavola • 280

Soufflé, Le • 268
Square Trousseau, Le • 280

T
Tante Louise • 277
Train Bleu, Le • 280
Trou Gascon, Au • 280

V
Vieux Chêne, Au • 278

W
Willi's Wine Bar • 268

Z
Zygomates, Les • 281

MARKET INDEX

A

Aguesseau Open-Air Food Market / Le Marché Aguesseau • 110

Alésia Open-Air Food Market / Le Marché Alésia • 170

Alibert Open-Air Food Market / Le Marché Alibert • 141

Amiral Bruix Open-Air Food Market / Le Marché Amiral Bruix • 220

Antiquarian and Used Book Market /
    Le Marché du Livre Ancien et d'Occasion • 211

Antiques Courtyard / La Cour des Antiquaires • 114

Anvers Open-Air Food Market / Le Marché Anvers • 125

Artisan Bakers and Artisan Foods • 77

Auguste-Blanqui Open-Air Food Market / Le Marché Auguste-Blanqui • 171

Auteuil Antiques Village / Halle d'Auteuil • 224

Auteuil Open-Air Food Market / Le Marché Auteuil • 220

B

Baltard, Victor, Architect • 139
Barbès Open-Air Food Market / Le Marché Barbès • 233
Bastille Art and Crafts Market / Le Marché de la Création Bastille • 152
Bastille Open-Air Food Market (also known as Richard Lenoir) /
    Le Marché Bastille • 145
Batignolles Covered Food Market / Le Marché Couvert Batignolles • 226
Batignolles Organic Open-Air Food Market /
    Le Marché Biologique des Batignolles • 105, 226
Baudoyer Open-Air Food Market / Le Marché Baudoyer • 52
Beauvau Covered Food Market / Le Marché Couvert Beauvau • 155
Belgrand Open-Air Food Market / Le Marché Belgrand • 256
Belleville Open-Air Food Market / Le Marché Belleville • 148
Bercy Open-Air Food Market / Le Marché Bercy • 162
Berthier Open-Air Food Market / Le Marché Berthier • 227
Bobillot Open-Air Food Market / Le Marché Bobillot • 174
Bon Marché Gourmet Food Hall / La Grande Épicerie au Bon Marché • 89
Book and Paper Market / Le Marché aux Vieux Papiers • 261
Booksellers on the Seine / Les Bouquinistes • 41, 52, 86
Bourse Open-Air Food Market / Le Marché Bourse • 37
Brancusi Organic Open-Air Food Market /
    Le Marché Biologique Brancusi • 188
Brassens Open-Air Food Market / Le Marché Brassens • 203
Breads, Artisan and Artisan Bakers • 77
Brocante Fairs • 246
Brune Open-Air Food Market / Le Marché Brune • 190

C

Cervantes Open-Air Food Market / Le Marché Cervantes • 203
La Chapelle Covered Food Market / Le Marché Couvert Chapelle • 237
Charonne Open-Air Food Market / Le Marché Charonne • 150
Clignancourt Flea Market /
    Le Marché aux Puces de Saint-Ouen—Clignancourt • 243
Convention Open-Air Food Market / Le Marché Convention • 204
Cooking in Paris • 38

Cours de Vincennes Open-Air Food Market /
     Le Marché Cours de Vincennes • 163
Covered Fish Market – Samurais of the Seas /
     Halle aux Poissons – Les Samouraïs des Mers • 205
Covered Passages / Les Passages Couverts • 45, 127
Crimée-Curial Open-Air Food Market / Le Marché Crimée Curial • 250

D

Daumesnil Open-Air Food Market / Le Marché Daumesnil • 164
Davout Open-Air Food Market / Le Marché Davout • 256
Drouot Montaigne Auction House / L'Hôtel Drouot Montaigne • 115
Drouot Richelieu Auction House / L'Hôtel Drouot Richelieu • 131

E

Eating Out in Paris • 263
Edgar Quinet Arts and Crafts Market /
     Le Marché de la Création Edgar Quinet • 179
Edgar Quinet Open-Air Food Market / Le Marché Edgar Quinet • 193
Enfants Rouges Covered Food Market /
     Le Marché Couvert Enfants Rouges • 50

F

Flower and Bird Markets, The /
     Les Marchés aux Fleurs et aux Oiseaux Cité • 53
Food Markets, Getting Along in the • 17

G

Galeries Lafayette Gourmet Food Hall / Galeries Lafayette Gourmet • 119
Grenelle Open-Air Food Market / Le Marché Grenelle • 201
Gros-la-Fontaine Open-Air Food Market / Le Marché Gros-la-Fontaine • 221

J

Jean Jaurès Open-Air Food Market / Le Marché Jean Jaurès • 250
Jeanne d'Arc Open-Air Food Market / Le Marché Jeanne d'Arc • 174
Joinville Open-Air Food Market / Le Marché Joinville • 251

L

Lecourbe Open-Air Food Market / Le Marché Lecourbe • 208
Ledru-Rollin Open-Air Food Market / Le Marché Ledru-Rollin • 164
Lefevbre Open-Air Food Market / Le Marché Lefevbre • 208
Left Bank Art and Antiques / Le Carré Rive Gauche • 101
Les Halles Underground Shopping Center • 31
Louvre of Antiques Dealers / Le Louvre des Antiquaires • 27
Louvre Underground Shopping Center • 27

M

Maison-Blanche Open-Air Food Market / Marché Maison-Blanche • 175
Markets, Virtual and Market Streets • 122
Maubert Open-Air Food Market / Le Marché Maubert-Mutualité • 69
Mortier Open-Air Food Market / Le Marché Mortier • 257
Mouton-Duvernet Open-Air Food Market (also known as Montrouge) /
    Le Marché Mouton-Duvernet • 186

N

Navier Open-Air Food Market / Le Marché Navier • 227
Ney Open-Air Food Market / Le Marché Ney • 239

O

Open on Sunday • 288
Ordener Open-Air Food Market / Le Marché Ordener • 240
Organic, Buying • 108
Ornano Open-Air Food Market / Le Marché Ornano • 240
Oysters, About • 92

P

Paris Rive Gauche Open-Air Food Market / Le Marché Paris Rive Gauche • 175
Passy Covered Food Market / Le Marché Couvert Passy • 222
Père-Lachaise Open-Air Food Market / Le Marché Père-Lachaise • 257
Place de la Madeleine Flower Market / Le Marché aux Fleurs Madeleine • 116
Place des Fêtes Open-Air Food Market / Le Marché Place des Fêtes • 253
Place des Ternes Flower Market / Le Marché aux Fleurs Ternes • 230

Place Monge Open-Air Food Market / Le Marché Monge • 61
Point du Jour Open-Air Food Market / Le Marché Point du Jour • 222
Poniatowski Open-Air Food Market / Le Marché Poniatowski • 165
Popincourt Open-Air Food Market / Le Marché Popincourt • 151
Port Royal Open-Air Food Market / Le Marché Port Royal • 70
Porte Brunet Open-Air Food Market / Le Marché Porte Brunet • 253
Porte d'Aubervilliers Open-Air Food Market /
     Le Marché Porte d'Aubervilliers • 254
Porte de Montreuil Flea Market / Le Marché aux Puces de Montreuil • 263
Porte de Vanves Flea Market /
     Le Marché aux Puces de la Porte de Vanves • 195
Porte Molitor Open-Air Food Market / Le Marché Porte Molitor • 223
Postage Stamp and Telephone Card Markets /
     Le Marché des Timbres (de la Philatélie) • 111
Président Wilson Open-Air Food Market / Le Marché Président Wilson • 215
Pyrénées Open-Air Food Market / Le Marché Pyrénées • 258

R

Raspail Open-Air Food Market / Le Marché Raspail • 73
Raspail Organic Open-Air Food Market / Le Marché Biologique Raspail • 81
Reunion Open-Air Food Market / Le Marché Reunion • 258
Rue Cadet Market Street / La Rue Cadet • 126
Rue Cler Market Street / La Rue Cler • 94
Rue d'Aligre Market Street / Le Marché Rue d'Aligre • 159
Rue Daguerre Market Street / La Rue Daguerre • 191
Rue de l'Annonciation Market Street / Rue de l'Annonciation • 223
Rue de Levis Market Street / La Rue de Levis • 229
Rue Dejean Market Street / La Rue Dejean • 241
Rue du Poteau-Rue Duhesme Market Street /
     La Rue du Poteau-Rue Duhesme Marketplaces • 242
Rue Montorgueil Market Street / La Rue Montorgueil • 35
Rue Mouffetard Market Street / La Rue Mouffetard • 65
Rue Poncelet Market Street / La Rue Poncelet • 229
Rungis Wholesale Market / Les Halles de Rungis • 181

S

Saint-Charles Open-Air Food Market / Le Marché Saint-Charles • 209
Saint-Didier Covered Food Market / Le Marché Couvert Saint-Didier • 224
Saint-Eloi Open-Air Food Market / Le Marché Saint-Eloi • 165
Saint-Eustache Les Halles Open-Air Food Market /
    Le Marché Saint-Eustache Les Halles • 24
Saint-Germain Art and Antiques Galleries /
    Le Carré des Arts Saint-Germain • 86
Saint-Germain Covered Food Market /
    Le Marché Couvert Saint-Germain-des-Prés • 85
Saint Honoré Antiques Village / Le Village Saint-Honoré • 28
Saint-Honoré Open-Air Food Market / Le Marché Saint-Honoré • 25
Saint-Martin Covered Food Market / Le Marché Couvert Saint Martin • 142
Saint-Paul Antiques Village / Le Village Saint-Paul • 57
Saint-Pierre Fabric Market / Le Marché Saint-Pierre • 247
Saint-Quentin Covered Food Market / Le Marché Couvert Saint-Quentin • 137
Salpêtrière Open-Air Food Market / Le Marché Salpêtrière • 176
Saxe-Breteuil Open-Air Food Market / Le Marché Saxe-Breteuil • 97
Swiss Village Antiques / Le Village Suisse • 102

T

Taste, in Search of Superior • 213
Télégraphe Open-Air Food Market / Le Marché Télégraphe • 259
Ternes Covered Food Market / Le Marché Couvert Ternes • 228
Treilhard Covered Food Market (formerly Marché Europe) /
    Le Marché Couvert • 110

V

Viaduct Arts and Crafts Shops / Le Viaduc des Arts • 167
Villemain Open-Air Food Market / Le Marché Villemain • 192
Villette Open-Air Food Market / Le Marché de la Villette • 254
Vincent Auriol Open-Air Food Market / Le Marché Vincent Auriol • 176

Acknowledgments

We especially wish to thank Iwonka Kelly and Michael Tushman whose contributions can be read between nearly every line. Iwonka's attention to the French language and her familiarity with Paris improved the book's accuracy. Michael enthusiastically immersed himself in the markets alongside Marjorie, bringing his well-honed observational skills to bear on a new organizational dynamic. Market outings became the daily routine for six months, enriching not only mealtimes but their entire adventure in Paris.

Both authors are grateful to Angela Hederman at The Little Bookroom for her superb matchmaking, keen judgment, and unflagging support. If all publishers handled authors as well as Angela does, the industry would be a happier place. Our thanks too to others who have been instrumental in bringing this new edition "to market": Marni Clippinger, Carol Franco, Beth Grossman, Rob Frankel, Robin Heyden, Debbie Gabrielle, Anthony Khoi, Rachel Tushman, Maggie and Jonathan Tushman, Roland Grin, Sandy Tilton, Sidne Koenigsberg, Young Park, Marla Felcher, Frances Levin, Brian Pfeiffer, Betty Rosbottom, Mimi Reeder, Leslie Zheutlin, and the Resonancy Writers.

About the Authors

Michael Tischman

Dixon Long is the author, along with Ruthanne Long, of the first edition of *Markets of Paris* and of *Markets of Provence*. He is also a novelist and short story writer, as well as dean emeritus and professor emeritus of political science at Case Western Reserve University. He has lived in Paris and Provence.

Marjorie R. Williams has been attending farmers markets since her childhood. Her work has been featured in *Edible* magazine and travel blogs. She has an MFA in creative writing and held executive editorial positions with major publishers. She also writes short fiction and is a book coach. She and her husband have lived in Paris and reside in Cambridge, Massachusetts.